Selective Responsibility
in the United Nations

Kilombo: International Relations and Colonial Questions

Series Editors: Mustapha K. Pasha, Aberystwyth University, Meera Sabaratnam, SOAS University of London, and Robbie Shilliam, Queen Mary University of London

This is the first series to mark out a dedicated space for advanced critical inquiry into colonial questions across international relations (IR). The ethos of this book series is reflected by the bricolage constituency of Kilombos—settlements of African slaves, rebels, and indigenous peoples in South America who became self-determining political communities that retrieved and renovated the social practices of its diverse constituencies while being confronted by colonial forces. The series embraces a multitude of methods and approaches, theoretical and empirical scholarship, alongside historical and contemporary concerns. Publishing innovative and top quality peer-reviewed scholarship, Kilombo enquires into the shifting principles of colonial rule that inform global governance and investigates the contestation of these principles by diverse peoples across the globe. It critically reinterprets popular concepts, narratives, and approaches in the field of IR by reference to the "colonial question," and, in doing so, the book series opens up new vistas from which to address the key political questions of our time.

Titles in the Series:

Selective Responsibility in the United Nations

Colonial Histories and Critical Inquiry

Katy Harsant

ROWMAN & LITTLEFIELD
Lanham • Boulder • New York • London

Published by Rowman & Littlefield
An imprint of The Rowman & Littlefield Publishing Group, Inc.
4501 Forbes Boulevard, Suite 200, Lanham, Maryland 20706
www.rowman.com

86-90 Paul Street, London EC2A 4NE

British Library Cataloguing in Publication Information Available

Library of Congress Cataloging-in-Publication Data

Names: Harsant, Katy, author.
Title: Selective responsibility in the United Nations : colonial histories and
    critical inquiry / Katy Harsant.
Description: Lanham : Rowman & Littlefield, [2022] | Series: Kilombo : international
    relations and colonial questions | Includes bibliographical references and index.
Identifiers: LCCN 2022023340 (print) | LCCN 2022023341 (ebook) |
    ISBN 9781786610287 (cloth) | ISBN 9781538172971 (paperback) |
    ISBN 9781786610300 (ebook)
Subjects: LCSH: United Nations—History. | United Nations. Security Council. |
    Sovereignty. | Postcolonialism. | Eurocentrism. | Administrative responsibility. |
    Intervention (International law) | Security, International.
Classification: LCC JZ4986 .H37 2022 (print) | LCC JZ4986 (ebook) |
    DDC 341.2309—dc23/eng/20220801
LC record available at https://lccn.loc.gov/2022023340
LC ebook record available at https://lccn.loc.gov/2022023341

For Stanley

Contents

Acknowledgements

This book has been in the works for many years, featuring some happy interruptions, such as the birth of my son, and some less happy interruptions, not least a global pandemic. It is in this context that I acknowledge the support of a vast number of people – too many to name here – without whom this would not have been possible.

For believing in the project and their endless patience, my deepest thanks go to the series editors, Robbie Shilliam, Meera Sabaratnam and Mustapha K. Pasha. I am particularly grateful to Robbie for his detailed and thoughtful comments on the entire manuscript. I must also thank Dhara Snowden, Rebecca Anastasi, Michael Kerns and Elizabeth Von Buhr from Rowman & Littlefield for their guidance on the publishing process and understanding the juggle.

This project began life as a PhD thesis and so I express my gratitude to my supervisors, Gurminder K. Bhambra and Goldie Osuri, for their guidance in its early stages, as well as Olivia Rutazibwa and Alice Mah for being the most encouraging-while-critical examiners I could have wished for. My students, colleagues and friends at Warwick Sociology have provided inspiration and support in more ways than they know. I am particularly indebted to Akwugo Emejulu and Sivamohan Valluvan for their advice, coffee and recommendations of detective novels to see me through the writing process.

Personal thanks go to Tiffany Anderson, Emily McCrea and Chloe Steele for being my ultimate cheerleaders and never losing enthusiasm. My family is entirely bemused by my job but is proud nonetheless and has provided love, support and free childcare, so thank you to my parents, siblings and my rowdy rabble of nieces and nephews. And of course, always, to Bill and Stanley for giving me a home so full of love and laughter, even on the worst days.

Abbreviations

HPPPDA	History and Public Policy Programme Digital Archive
ICISS	International Commission on Intervention and State Sovereignty
IISH	International Institute of Social History (Amsterdam)
LAIA	League against Imperialism Archives
NAM	Non-Aligned Movement
UN	United Nations
UNCIO	United Nations Conference on International Organisation

Introduction

Selective Responsibility and Reading through History

The early years of the 2010s saw a wave of anti-government protests in the Middle East and North Africa – often referred to as the 'Arab Spring' – which resulted in significant large-scale military conflicts in the region. As an institution of global governance, the United Nations was duty bound to respond, and yet it became rapidly apparent that its principles and policies were not applied evenly in all contexts. In Libya, for example, the United Nations adopted Resolution 1973 in 2011, authorising international forces to use 'all necessary measures' to protect Libyan civilians (United Nations Security Council, 2011). The United Nations concluded that the Libyan government had committed extensive human rights violations in response to protestors, as well as failing to comply with earlier warnings from the Security Council (Çakmak 2019). To authorise humanitarian military intervention in any context, the United Nations relies on the concept of *responsibility*. Intervention is deemed necessary or appropriate based on the *responsibility* of the international community to respond when civilians are in danger, and this is explicit in the policy of Responsibility to Protect (or R2P), which was adopted by the United Nations in 2005. The actions of the United Nations in relation to intervention are grounded in an understanding of the organisation as an international community of states and led by its primary aim of protecting international peace and security (United Nations 1945). In authorising intervention in Libya, the United Nations claimed to be acting on the responsibility of the international community to protect innocent civilians. However, despite replicating the Libyan context in many ways, the concurrent war in Syria saw no such response. Protestors were met with a violent response by government forces, and violations of international law were documented by the Human Rights Council and Human Rights Watch (Çakmak 2019). Yet no intervention was authorised, despite meeting the relevant criteria under

1

United Nations policy. It is this differential response to conflict, particularly in terms of intervention, that provided the provocation for this book: How is it possible that the United Nations intervenes in some cases and not others? How is it possible for responsibility to be applied selectively?

Despite its rhetoric and claims to universality, in practice, the United Nations is an organisation that is dominated by five states with significant global power, namely the five permanent members of the Security Council – the United Kingdom, the United States, France, China and Russia. The Security Council holds primary responsibility for responding to events that threaten international peace and security, and so it is these five states who ultimately decide whether to intervene or not. The issue of selectivity has been apparent in the activities of the Security Council since its establishment in 1945 across a range of conflicts and is in large part caused by the right of the permanent members to veto, whereby any one of the five can prevent action through a negative vote. While the Security Council also includes ten non-permanent members, who serve terms of two years each, these members do not have the right to veto and so cannot prevent action if there is otherwise a majority. In the case of Syria noted above, intervention has been prevented by Russia and China consistently utilising their right to veto (Rotmann et al. 2014). This power and privilege afforded to the permanent five members of the Security Council are again grounded in a narrative of responsibility, whereby these five states carry a particular burden for maintaining international peace and security. The focus on *selective* responsibility here is to emphasise that this responsibility is not objective or neutral. The moral connotations of the term responsibility are wielded when required to justify the actions of the Security Council, but the structures in place enable a relinquishment of this responsibility where states deem it appropriate or preferable to their interests.

In exploring the idea of selective responsibility in the United Nations, the chapters that follow demonstrate the ways in which the concept of responsibility in the context of international relations is deeply embedded within histories of colonisation and associated worldviews. The structural organisation of the United Nations reinforces and perpetuates understandings of race, civilisation, development, and sovereignty that have their roots in colonialism and colonial power dynamics. This book, therefore, seeks to challenge the dominant narratives of equality and progress that surround the United Nations and show that it is, and always has been, an institution committed to the perpetuation of unequal power relations. To do so, the book foregrounds archival material from a range of sources, illuminating a long history of anti-colonial resistance both internal and external to the United Nations, as well as engaging with scholars who have provided anti-colonial critiques of the United Nations and international law more broadly. The book begins and ends with the question of military intervention as a means of explaining the importance of locating contemporary debates within their broader historical context, that is, reading through history. In order to answer the question posed here – how is it possible that the United Nations responds with intervention in some contexts and not others? – we need to understand the structures in place, which in turn requires an examination of the history of the United Nations and how those structures came to be.

POSTCOLONIALISM, NEOCOLONIALISM AND SOVEREIGNTY

While there remains a commitment in the popular imaginary to understand colonialism as something that happened in the past, the arguments made here draw on postcolonial theory, which seeks to disrupt dominant discourses that naturalise the asymmetrical and disadvantageous development of the globe that occurred as a result of colonialism and imperialism (see, for example, Bhabha 1994; Fanon 1965; Rodney 2012 [1972]). Central to this is the understanding that colonialism did not end with the granting of independence to former colonial territories, as colonialism shaped the world to such a degree that its influence cannot be undone through the formal political process of decolonisation. This book's focus on the United Nations highlights the ways in which international institutions contribute to what Gandhi calls the 'mystifying amnesia of the colonial aftermath' (1998, 4) by reproducing a narrative of colonialism as a historical event that has since been overcome. The examination of archival material illustrates the ways in which the colonial history of the United Nations has affected its very foundations, its structures and its ways of framing the world, while noting that this colonial history is virtually absent from the commonly accepted historical narrative of its founding. The United Nations and colonialism are mostly seen as two separate entities, while the archives show that they are inextricably linked.

Although postcolonial theory provides the lens through which the problem is viewed, throughout the following chapters, distinctions will be made between 'postcolonial power' and 'neocolonial technologies of power'. References to 'postcolonial power' signify an acknowledgement that colonialism affected the structure of global society to the extent that we cannot understand the current positioning of states without understanding their role in, or relationship to, colonialism. The use of this term represents an acknowledgement that while most states have undergone a process of formal decolonisation, the effects of colonialism are so significant that we must continue to recognise its impact when discussing the contemporary global context (Seth 2013). This term will therefore be used when discussing colonial power structures that continue to dominate contemporary relationships between states. The concepts of neocolonialism and neocolonial technologies refer to something slightly different. Writing in the years following the decolonisation of large parts of Africa, Nkrumah (1965) argues that neocolonialism developed as the main instrument of imperialism following the granting of independence to the colonies, operating through economic or financial control. Neocolonialism, therefore, refers to the practices of former imperial powers that result in the economic control of colonies that have been granted independence. These practices are often developed as part of the process of decolonisation via international law and international institutions (Anghie 2005). Within the context of this book, the terms 'neocolonialism' or 'neocolonial technologies' will be used in order to refer to the mechanisms developed through the process of decolonisation that allows imperial powers to maintain control over colonial territories despite granting formal (i.e. political) independence. These practices cannot be referred to as colonial as they do not form part of a relationship of direct rule by one state over another, rather they are *neo*colonial as they were developed as *new* ways of maintaining control following independence. As Nkrumah argues: 'The question is one of power. A State in the grips of neocolonialism is not master of its own destiny' (1965: x).

Linked to this is the question of sovereignty, which is perhaps the most significant political concept for the United Nations, with the founding documents making frequent reference to the sovereignty of member states as fundamental to the organisation (United Nations 1945). While these governing documents frame sovereignty as simply the right of a state to govern itself, this book will demonstrate the ways in which both the concept of sovereignty and international law, more broadly, are powerful tools in maintaining colonial power dynamics, particularly in terms of mediating relationships between Western and non-Western states. Drawing on Third World Approaches to International Law (TWAIL) (e.g. Anghie 2001; Rajagopal 2003), this book asserts that sovereignty emerges as a means of justifying colonisation and enforcing European culture as universal culture through frameworks of development and progress. These approaches to understanding international law, used in conjunction with a broader postcolonial lens, help to explain how the West has managed to ensure the institutionalisation of colonial power dynamics within systems of global governance and the United Nations more specifically.

Taken together, these theoretical frameworks are deployed in the chapters that follow to explain how selective responsibility within the United Nations is made possible. To understand how selective responsibility operates, it is necessary to explore the structures that enable it and the logics that underpin those structures. Postcolonial theory helps to show that the power and position of the permanent members of the Security Council are bound up in the logics of colonialism, whereby they are understood to be *naturally* more advanced, more developed and, thus, more responsible for maintaining peace and security on a global scale. It explains the enduring legacy of colonisation in creating and sustaining global hierarchies of power politically, economically and socially. Following on from this, the concept of neocolonialism reveals how the United Nations has developed new systems of control to maintain these hierarchies following the formal process of decolonisation. Thinking specifically about the question of intervention, the concept of neocolonialism helps to illuminate the ways in which intervening states influence the political, economic and social structures of a country in crisis to maintain existing global hierarchies. This, in turn, demonstrates the complexities and contradictions inherent in the United Nations' focus on *responsibility* as the underlying motivation for intervention. When the Security Council authorises intervention under the policy of Responsibility to Protect, it is saying that the state in question has forfeited its right to sovereignty (i.e. to govern itself) on the basis of a violation of international law or some other breach of international peace. However, when we consider the colonial origins of the concept of sovereignty, it becomes clear that sovereignty is not a neutral concept, equally available to all states. These theoretical frameworks are weaved through the pages that follow to establish the significance of understanding the colonial origins of the United Nations for understanding contemporary questions around how it operates, pushing us to read contemporary debates through their historical origins.

READING THROUGH HISTORY

Sabaratnam defines Eurocentrism as 'the sensibility that *Europe is historically, economically, culturally and politically distinctive in ways which significantly determine the overall character of world politics*' (emphasis in original) (2017, 20). Eurocentrism works on the basis that Europe is and has been historically the centre of world politics and that, as such, our analysis should begin from the perspective of Europe. This idea has been persistent in the social sciences, where the modern world – characterised by industrialisation, democracy and secularisation – is seen as a European invention that has or will slowly spread out to the rest of the world (Bhambra 2007). In the context of this book, Eurocentrism explains the production of particular historical 'facts' about the United Nations and is central to the discourses that enable the reproduction of colonial power dynamics. Foregrounding the work of anti-colonial groups throughout history in the chapters that follow represents an attempt to challenge Eurocentrism in our understanding of the

United Nations and its activities. International relations as an academic discipline has a tendency towards Eurocentrism, seeing Europe or the West as the primary focus of analysis and non-Western states as secondary objects of analysis (Sabaratnam 2017). The archival material displayed throughout this book demonstrates that politics happens outside of the West and the reconstruction of historical narratives surrounding the United Nations is an attempt to counteract the silencing or erasure of this.

The core focus of this project is theoretical, in providing a deconstruction of dominant narratives and the provision of an alternative discourse that may affect the way in which we understand contemporary debates within the United Nations. As such, this book is not engaging in a large-scale secondary analysis of documentary evidence in the way that social science research often does. Rather, historical documents from a range of archives feature as part of the process of de-silencing the narratives of resistance that have been silenced throughout history and as part of the process of reconstructing a history of the United Nations that takes this colonial and anti-colonial history into account. These archival documents are central to doing the work of de-silencing and deconstructing the dominant narrative that is both inaccurate and insufficient. This data ranges from official documents, such as the Charter of the United Nations, to minutes of meetings, letters between representatives from the United Nations and interested parties, and statements by anti-colonial groups, all used with the aim of providing evidence and bringing to life the arguments being made throughout the book, grounding them in the reality of the historical context.

A large majority of the archival data used as illustrative material comes from the United Nations' own archives, which sit in a small building on a side road a few minutes' walk from the main headquarters in New York. As a public body, the United Nations maintains records of its activities, a large proportion of which are now digitised and made available online, but the particular set relating to the 1945 conference in San Francisco is not. These documents were accessed on an in-person visit to the archives following correspondence with an archivist who provided an extensive list of documents that might have been relevant following a short description of the project. They were categorised in some cases by country (e.g. files relating to China or to India), in some cases by topic (e.g. 'Correspondence Files – Outgoing Letters – Minorities'), and in other cases more broadly (e.g. files related to the organisation of the conference). I booked a desk in the reading room and having filled out the relevant forms and received warnings about pens and confusing the order of the files, the requested files were brought out three at a time for me to look through. The process of finding and accessing these documents is important to discuss here as it represents a range of wider issues related to creating and using archives, as well as studying history, which will be addressed shortly. Documents from other archives referenced here (i.e. the League against Imperialism, the Bandung Conference, the Non-Aligned Movement and the Group of 77) were accessed online, which raises its own different obstacles. The use of archival data within this book has two primary objectives: firstly, providing an alternative or counter-narrative to the history that the United Nations tells of its own beginnings and, secondly, evidencing and remembering a long history of anti-colonial resistance to the United Nations. Each of these objectives raises interesting and important issues for scholars of the United Nations and international relations more broadly around historiography, power and the reproduction of inequality on a global scale.

Much has been written on the archive as a space of political power – not least Foucault's (2002 [1972]) *Archaeology of Knowledge* – that it is not necessary to review here lest this book double in size. However, there are a few key issues that relate more specifically to the kinds of data used in this book that help us to think about the significance of the archive for our understanding of contemporary debates. Firstly, an acknowledgement that archives are not objective historical records or non-political spaces for the storage of historical documents and they necessarily involve absences in a variety of ways. The process of archiving and using the archive as a basis for the production of knowledge about the past cannot be understood as a straightforward matter of recording/preserving/storing facts. For Trouillot, the creation of silences is a key aspect of the production of history and historical narratives that happens at four key moments:

> the moment of fact creation (the making of sources); the moment of fact assembly (the making of archives); the moment of fact retrieval (the making of narratives); and the moment of retrospective significance (the making of history in the final instance). (1995, 26)

Archival documents go through a process of selection – and selectivity – at all stages. For example, in the context of the United Nations archives, somebody decided what was worth noting down in a meeting, what was sensitive 'off the record' information, and which letters were worth preserving. Somebody else collated those documents and decided on a common theme by which to categorise them, based on their understanding of the organisation. The documents were put into a certain order within the files and listed in a catalogue. The archivist decided which elements of the catalogue would be helpful for my project based on a brief – and deliberately unpolitical – description. All of these decisions have an impact on the availability of knowledge about the past, and these are decisions made by human beings who are, in turn, influenced by their own positionality.

These aspects of archival production are important to note, although somewhat inevitable in the sense that human beings are involved in all stages of
the process and they have to make decisions about what and how to archive.
However, what is most interesting and significant for this book is the making
of narratives. In telling its own history, the United Nations leaves out particular elements of conflict and resistance that were present, as evidenced in its
own archives. In telling this history in the present and choosing to leave out
these elements, the United Nations creates silences through assigning retrospective significance only to the discussions between the major powers and
relegating the discussion of the colonial question to the status of minor issues.
The potential reasons for doing so are varied and have perhaps changed over
time, ranging from a conscious and politically motivated desire to underplay
the role of anti-colonial movements, resistance and sentiment in the interests
of ensuring the success of the United Nations in the early years, to a subcon-
scious and deeply ingrained belief that these were the 'important issues' and
colonialism was less so.

   What is being challenged here then is the idea of history as an objective fact.
At each stage of writing history, decisions are made about the authenticity of
particular 'facts' over others. History is not recorded but *produced* through
the continual privileging of certain accounts and the silencing of others, in
the creation of facts, the making of archives, the making of narratives and in
the acknowledgement of retrospective significance (Trouillot 1995). At each
of these points, the dominance of particular narratives gains more strength,
and the silencing of alternative narratives intensifies. To approach history in
this way is an acknowledgement of the place of power in narrating history,
particularly in relation to colonialism. Not all stories are told, not all people
have the power to tell stories, and only the stories of some come to be
understood as historical facts. Within the context of global history, it is the
history of the West that is relentlessly reinforced as the universal history of
all (Bhambra 2007), and this project, alongside others, provides a challenge
to that. In addition to being ascribed the status of objective fact, history is
understood to be a process of remembering the past, and historians are often
characterised as those who are responsible for preserving it. However, history
is not only a process of remembering but also a process of forgetting. History
involves the selection and the preservation of particular aspects of the past,
with the simultaneous forgetting or silencing of other aspects deemed less
important. The narratives that are preserved come to be known as 'facts',
and the narratives that are silenced are forgotten, no longer existing in our
collective memory of the past. The process of forgetting is particularly
significant in relation to the dominance of imperial narratives of history (see
Morefield 2014). The aim of this book is to provide a history of resistance
that was ultimately accompanied by a history of domination to challenge the

dominant narratives of equality and progress that allow the major powers to disguise the perpetuation of imperial power within the United Nations. In doing so, it provides an example of the importance of listening to 'counter-discourses' that are often obscured by the Eurocentric claims of Western history to be representing universal history (Morefield 2014). By exploring the histories of those dominated by the world's major powers, it is possible to illuminate the extent to which postcolonial privilege has allowed for the universalisation of European values and the way that histories of the powerful have come to represent the history of the world.

Making use of anti-colonial archives is, therefore, an important way in which to challenge the collective forgetting of particular elements of global history. It is key to ensuring that we understand the continued significance of colonialism for the contemporary structure of the world and how the United Nations operates. However, in addition to the issues of selectivity outlined above that affect all archives, anti-colonial archives face another set of problems related to their transnationality. As Jones (2017) has argued, anti-colonial archives are affected by the same problem that confronts anti-colonial struggles more broadly in that they necessarily span a wide geographical space, and so generating a collection of material items is incredibly difficult. While the activities of the United Nations that are recorded happen in a relatively small range of places, anti-colonial activity was and is a global project meaning that it is harder to assemble a coherent archive. The more recent digitisation of documents from anti-colonial movements has gone some way in making this material more accessible, but this is a long-term project.

The chapters of this book are written in the spirit of remembrance as a means of challenging the process of forgetting that is central to the production of dominant historical narratives. The book acknowledges that the key to challenging dominant narratives is to remember alternative narratives and stories. This does not mean that we should simply tell other stories and let them coexist but that we must use other narratives to identify the holes in the dominant narrative. As Grovogui (2016) argues, revisiting and remembering are not only about establishing the inaccuracies of existing narratives but also central to *reconstructing* those narratives. The aim is not to allow existing narratives to stand while adding these forgotten moments to them, but to reconstruct them and assess how we might understand the world differently if we take these moments seriously and understand the connections. In the context of Grovogui's (2016) recollection of Bandung, remembering this political moment serves not only to challenge the West's ownership of the norms of contemporary international relations but also to argue that norms were also created in non-Western spaces and by non-Western actors. To remember these moments is to recognise the contributions of non-Western political actors and acknowledge their significance in spite of disciplinary traditions and narratives that seek to exclude them.

Much work has been done in recent years – and as part of the much longer academic project of postcolonial thinking – to address the role of colonialism and to critique Eurocentrism in our understanding of the modern world. In the academic field of international relations (IR), where this book most comfortably sits, this has arguably been the domain of so-called critical IR, which has been allowed to coexist with mainstream IR but without doing much to alter it. For Pasha (2016), this problem is the result of the simultaneous interdisciplinarity and the transdisciplinarity of decolonial thinking. Decolonial thinking goes beyond the boundaries of Western knowledge systems, which are structured around the enlightenment assertion that knowledge begins in Europe and spreads out to the rest of the world. Western knowledge systems produce disciplinary regimes and boundaries, whereas decolonial thinking links elements of many disciplines together and goes beyond the boundaries of academic knowledge production to include people as key actors and stakeholders. As such, the task for Critical IR scholars is to connect critiques of Eurocentrism to a decolonial archive, which demonstrates that alternative ways of thinking and being exist and have existed outside of the West and outside of the academy (Pasha 2016).

The core premise of this book is that in order to understand contemporary global problems, it is necessary to read them through their historical origins. Within the specific context of the United Nations, the book challenges the framing of the United Nations as an organisation with the primary aims of maintaining international peace and security and achieving international cooperation. It provides a postcolonial critique of the United Nations as an institution, particularly in relation to its claims to equality, with a focus on the ways in which both the structures of the organisation and the discourses surrounding it allow for selective responsibility when dealing with conflict at an international level. The continuation of problematic discourses of development, progress, and responsibility is a result of the suppression of colonialism in the historical narratives of the United Nations. The structuring of the United Nations in line with colonial power dynamics with the major powers as 'leaders' who have a particular responsibility to ensure the 'development' of the world has served to maintain the existing global order and develop new forms of neocolonial control following decolonisation and independence, privileging Western culture and equating difference with underdevelopment. It is crucial to recognise here that these are not simply academic debates about the history of the United Nations and its relationship to imperialism. These historical narratives enable and legitimate the structuring of the organisation, which allows for the selective enforcement of policy (e.g. in relation to military intervention), which has very real, material and often fatal consequences.

The approach of reading through history is framed by a belief that how we understand the past is crucial for how we understand the world today and that if our understanding of the past is inaccurate, our understanding of the present will necessarily be inadequate (Bhambra 2007). The key idea underlying all of the chapters of this book and the argument that is built throughout is that it is inadequate to simply explore contemporary issues by examining their contemporary circumstances. To do so, fails to acknowledge the history of Western dominance that has legitimated power structures that allow for selective decision-making around intervention within the United Nations. Therefore, in order to more accurately understand the power structures affecting decisions being made around intervention, it is necessary to look at these contemporary decisions within the historical context of colonialism and postcolonial power structures.

Using this framework to understand contemporary issues within the United Nations contributes to the broader project of challenging Eurocentrism within international relations and the social sciences. As Sabaratnam argues, the tendency towards Eurocentrism in academic writing on international relations limits our capacity for understanding in three key ways: 'first, where politics is located; second, who knows about it; and third, what kinds of responses are thinkable' (2017, 22). Even accounts and work that are critical of Europe and imperialism can nevertheless reinforce Eurocentrism by focusing on Europe or the West as the centre of global politics and neglecting the fact that politics happen elsewhere. This, in turn, limits the capacity for providing alternatives and thinking beyond Western liberalism so that we are sometimes left with critique and little else. The role of critical IR then is to explore the politics that happen elsewhere and use this to reconstruct our understandings. It requires us to re-centre our analysis away from the West as the centre of modernity and any possibilities for 'progress'.

STRUCTURE OF THE BOOK

Chapter 1 expands on the argument outlined here that providing a reconsideration of the history of the United Nations is necessary in order to understand the way in which power functions within the United Nations today. It challenges the position that the United Nations is a novel institution established at the end of the Second World War. Instead, this chapter argues, as others have, that the United Nations emerged out of the failures of the League of Nations while maintaining its fundamental power structures (see Mazower 2009). The chapter begins by detailing the established historical

narrative of the United Nations, which is told by both the United Nations
itself and by historians of it. Although there have been critical accounts of
the United Nations in terms of its historical development, few of these make
the connections between the power of the permanent members of the Security
Council and their historical links to colonialism (some examples of those
that do are Anderson 2003, 2015; Sherwood 1996; Plummer 1996, 2003).
There is a tendency to view the United Nations as a new approach to world
politics, whether in a positive or negative light. This chapter argues against
this idea of rupture and shows that the United Nations is a rebranded League
of Nations rather than signifying a break with the League's power structures.
This chapter, therefore, provides the context for the archival material that will
be examined in the chapters that follow and summarises the position that is
being challenged. Making use of Third World Approaches to International
Law, this chapter also examines the concept of sovereignty as an organising
principle of the United Nations and how this features within colonial power
dynamics.

While chapter 1 outlines the context and what exactly the book is challenging in terms of dominant historical narratives, chapters 2 to 5 narrate a history
of resistance to colonial and neocolonial practices, highlighting the extent to
which the United Nations' claims to equality and universality are inaccurate
and problematic. These chapters foreground the long tradition of anti-colonial
resistance to and within global governance as a means of re-narrating the history of the United Nations and doing the work of reconstructing. Following
on from the argument outlined in chapter 1, chapter 2 examines the League of
Nations as the precursor to the United Nations, re-narrating its history to take
account of the resistance movements that challenged its power. The chapter
begins with the Paris Peace Conference of 1919 and US president Woodrow
Wilson's public advocacy of 'self-determination' as a core principle of
international relations in the run-up to the establishment of the League of
Nations. Despite Wilson's rhetoric, the early years of the League of Nations
demonstrated that this principle would not apply to colonised and formerly
colonised peoples and so chapter 2 examines the work of the League against
Imperialism, which was founded in 1927. Using archival material from the
League against Imperialism itself, this chapter provides a critique of the
concepts of universalism and internationalism that were frequently affirmed
by major powers within the League of Nations who were simultaneously
sustaining direct and indirect forms of colonial domination. The League
against Imperialism was a significant moment in anti-colonial resistance and
one that is often neglected in accounts of international organisations, and so
this chapter details the transnational solidarities that formed the basis of the
League against Imperialism and the issues that it addressed in terms of the
continuation of colonial oppression via the League of Nations.

Chapter 3 follows chronologically, detailing the founding of the United Nations after the League of Nations had been denounced as a failure. Inspired by Sherwood's (1996) observation that historical accounts of the United Nations neglect the efforts of black and anti-colonial activists to add decolonisation to the agenda in the formation of a new global organisation, this chapter provides an alternative historical narrative to those usually seen in academic scholarship. Making use of archival data from the United Nations' own archives, it examines the debates around the institutionalisation of colonial power dynamics, particularly in relation to the Security Council, that were very much present at the founding of the organisation in 1945. It brings texture to these academic debates through a close reading of archival material, detailing the specific discussions between individual state actors. In doing so, this chapter highlights the ways in which the structure of the organisation was contested at the time and the influence of Eurocentric discourses around development, progress and responsibility in justifying this structure.

Chapter 4 makes use of archival material from the Bandung Conference, which took place in 1955, ten years after the founding of the United Nations. The focus of Bandung was on cultivating solidarities between Asian and African states outside of the United Nations, grounded in the long tradition of transnational anti-colonial activism. The solidarities forged at Bandung and the discussions around political, economic and social issues provide evidence of international politics happening beyond and outside of the West, while also highlighting the ways in which existing and former colonies utilised the opportunities that the Cold War provided within the context of the United Nations in pushing for decolonisation. This chapter also examines the trusteeship system within the United Nations and how the language of development, progress and responsibility functions to maintain colonial power dynamics. Reading the details of Bandung and the trusteeship system together again provides us with a more multifaceted and complex narrative in relation to the history of the United Nations and its relationship to colonialism, reinforcing the arguments made earlier about the tendency to see Western politics as universal and non-Western politics as 'other', rather than as connected.

The United Nations adopted the Declaration on the Granting of Independence to Colonial Countries and Peoples in 1960, which many saw as the beginning of the end of colonialism. Chapter 5 maps out some of the key movements that have emerged since the Bandung conference and the 1960 Declaration, outlining their priorities and demands in terms of continuing to hold the major powers of the United Nations to account. It examines more recent statements from groups such as the Non-Aligned Movement and the Group of 77, which emphasise the continued impact of colonisation on the economic and political circumstances of formerly colonised states, providing a critique of the United Nations and the ongoing privileging of great power interests. This chapter brings the book into the present day and concludes the narration of a history of anti-colonial resistance that represents a challenge to the United Nations' own narrative.

Having demonstrated the historical persistence of colonial power dynamics through institutions of global governance from the League of Nations to the most recent years of the United Nations, chapter 6 clarifies the implications of this for contemporary debates, using the example of military intervention. It charts the shift from the principle of non-intervention as enshrined in the Charter to the current policy of Responsibility to Protect, which states that the international community has a duty to intervene where a state fails to protect its citizens. In doing so, this chapter argues that Responsibility to Protect is a neocolonial technology that draws on the colonial discourses identified in earlier chapters. This chapter returns firmly to the original question of selective responsibility, demonstrating the implications of the alternative historical narrative that has been explored throughout.

Chapter 7 concludes the book and addresses the implications for our understanding of what the United Nations is and how it functions, as well as pulling together the various arguments made to ask who is able write history and what happens to our understanding of the present if we re-narrate history to take seriously those who have been silenced. The notion of selective responsibility within the United Nations is a prompt for thinking through the historical processes that enable selectivity in an organisation that makes claims to universality, equality, and justice through adherence to international law. It encourages us to consider how some humanitarian crises can provoke military intervention and others not and the historical conditions that allow for this decision to be made (or action prevented) by just five states. Digging deeper into these questions, the prompt of selective responsibility uncovers a rich history of anti-colonial resistance within global governance that can aid us in reconstructing our understandings of how global governance works and what we must do to challenge the reproduction of inequality.

Chapter 1

From Sovereignty to Sovereign Equality

Although there have been numerous critical accounts of the United Nations in terms of its historical development, some of which are discussed here, few of these make the connections between the power of the permanent members of the Security Council and their historical links to colonial domination. There is a tendency to view the United Nations as a novel institution, whether in a positive or negative light. This chapter argues against this idea of rupture and instead follows Mark Mazower's (2009) claim that the United Nations was born out of 'evolution not revolution' in that it acts as a rebranded League of Nations rather than signifying a meaningful break with the League's power structures. The purpose of this chapter, therefore, is to establish both the theoretical framework of the book and the historiographical intervention being made. The chapter begins by detailing the established historical narrative of the United Nations, which is told by both the United Nations itself and by many historians of it. Following on from this, the chapter focuses on the concept of sovereignty and how it features in the grounding principles of the United Nations and earlier organisations. Drawing particularly upon Third World Approaches to International Law, it displays the ways in which international institutions have used the concept of sovereignty as a grounding principle while disguising its origins as a concept born out of the colonial encounter and the need to make sense of relationships between coloniser and colonised. The chapter employs this critique in dealing with the distinction between sovereignty and sovereign *equality* that was introduced by the United Nations to address the perceived problems of the League of Nations.

A central criticism of the League was that its protection of the sovereignty of states prevented meaningful action where it was required, and hence the United Nations claimed to be working on a principle of sovereign equality that respected the sovereignty of all states and their right to self-determination.

However, the argument here is that this concept of sovereign equality is inherently contradictory due to the roots of the concept of sovereignty itself. The chapter applies this critique in an examination of the United Nations system of trusteeship and the League of Nations mandate system. This develops the theoretical argument that is demonstrated throughout the rest of the book in terms of the failure of the United Nations to provide a system that is fundamentally different from what went before, which is mystified through claims to 'sovereign equality' without acknowledging the colonial history of sovereignty as an idea. It also establishes the centrality of responsibility as an organising principle for both the League and the United Nations, particularly within the systems designed to deal with colonial territories, and the ways that governing documents draw on a moral reasoning that obscures underlying colonial power dynamics.

A HISTORY OF THE UNITED NATIONS

The United Nations' history of its own existence tells a very particular story. Starting with a meeting between Winston Churchill and Franklin D. Roosevelt, it constructs a narrative of democratic progression from an initial commitment to common principles of peace to a formal pledge of global cooperation by 80 per cent of the world's population. This narrative focuses on the United Nations as a novel approach to international relations following the horrors of the Second World War and, as the result of free and open debate between all nations, signifying a united promise to prevent conflict. While it acknowledges that there were instances of tension and disagreement throughout the initial stages, it argues that these were dissolved through a process of negotiation and compromise in order to succeed in creating the organisation as it was envisaged.

As the United Nations is made up of an ever-increasing number of independent states that all play a role (to varying degrees) and all participate in the General Assembly, its decisions are commonly understood as the outcome of an international process of debate, negotiation and compromise. This process of debate, negotiation and cooperation that seemingly forms the basis of the United Nations results in the organisation itself being imbued with authority to deal with international issues above the authority of individual states, and this authority, in turn, results in a sense of legitimacy (Thakur 2006). Decisions made by the United Nations are seen to be decisions made by the international community, and this process of mutual deliberation that the United Nations claims to take part in leads to these decisions being understood as valid. The theoretically inclusive structure of the United Nations and its role as a cooperative organisation, as the culmination of competing interests, provides it with a sense of legitimacy that suggests that the things it says and does are accurate and in the general interest, rather than in the interests of individual states. It is for this reason that in providing an alternative historical narrative for the United Nations, the main focus here will be upon the history the United Nations tells of itself, as the sense of legitimacy afforded to the United Nations as an institution allows for its own narration of its history to be understood as factual and accurate.

The United Nations officially came into existence on 24 October 1945, following the ratification of the Charter. According to the narrative offered by the United Nations itself, this date represents the culmination of three years of negotiation between the world's major powers in the interests of developing a new organisation that would protect international peace and security. The Charter's preamble clearly states that the core aims of the United Nations as an international organisation are: to promote human rights, justice and social progress; to practice tolerance; and to maintain international peace and security. It emphasises the need to limit the use of armed force and makes a commitment to economic and social advancement for all people in the world. Ultimately, the United Nations was designed as an international agreement to prevent war on the scale that had been seen in the preceding six years. Its success and growth was reflective of the general mood following the Second World War: that something had to be done in order to prevent the conflict and loss of life on that scale from ever happening again. In signing the Charter, the original fifty-one member states declared an intention to act collectively to prevent war and to promote international peace and security, as well as to promote human rights and global advancement on all levels in order that the world would never again suffer as it had between 1939 and 1945.

The maintenance of international peace and security is and has always been a priority for the United Nations, and in affirming the primary purposes of the organisation the Charter states that this is to be delivered through cooperation, respect for human rights and dealing with acts of aggression through peaceful means. In addition, there is a focus on equality, respect and non-discrimination, reflecting upon the events of the Second World War. The absolute disregard for human rights shown by the Nazi regime had seemingly strengthened an international will for the development of a 'common law of mankind' that would allow for the protection of individuals from genocide (Goodwin 1971, 29). The United Nations was, in theory, to be based upon the fundamental human rights of all of the world's peoples and was designed to develop international standards of treatment as well as signify an agreement between states to prevent human rights abuse. This was further consolidated in the Universal Declaration of Human Rights in 1948, three years after the Charter of the United Nations was signed.

US president Franklin D. Roosevelt first used the name 'United Nations' in 1942, when representatives from twenty-six different nations pledged their allegiance and willingness to fight against the Axis powers of the Second World War, beginning the three-year period of negotiations (United Nations 2022a). However, the initial ideas of the United Nations as an institution are dated back to the signing of the Atlantic Charter by British prime minister Winston Churchill and Roosevelt in 1941. The two world leaders issued a joint statement of eight points following their meeting at sea, with the final point stating that:

> They believe all of the nations of the world, for realistic as well spiritual reasons, must come to the abandonment of the use of force. Since no future peace can be maintained if land, sea, or air armaments continue to be employed by nations which threaten, or may threaten aggression outside of their frontiers, they believe, pending the establishment of a wider and permanent system of general security, that the disarmament of such nations is essential. They will likewise aid and encourage all other practicable measures which will lighten for peace-loving peoples the crushing burden of armament. (Churchill and Roosevelt 1941)

The Atlantic Charter signified a commitment and desire by Britain and the United States to develop a widespread international system of security in order to deal with potential acts of aggression. The historical account provided by the United Nations argues that the Atlantic Charter encapsulated a novel agreement by these two leaders on common principles (United Nations 2022). This pledge was followed on New Year's Day of 1942 by the signing of the 'Declaration by United Nations', initially by Roosevelt, Churchill, Maxim Litvinov of the Soviet Union and T.V. Soong of China, and on 2 January by a further twenty-two nations committed to the principles outlined in the Atlantic Charter. The Atlantic Charter and the Declaration by United Nations are posed as the historical beginnings of the United Nations as we know it today, signifying an unprecedented dedication to principles of international peace and security.

The 1943 Moscow Conference is viewed as an attempt to ground this commitment to a peaceful world organisation in some sort of concrete structure, with the primary responsibility for its design falling to the leaders of the United Kingdom, the United States and the Soviet Union (United Nations 2022a). This meeting was followed by a declaration at the Tehran Conference in the same year, which stated that:

> And as to peace – we are sure that our concord will win an enduring Peace. We recognize fully the supreme responsibility resting upon us and all the United

Nations to make a peace which will command the goodwill of the overwhelming mass of the peoples of the world and banish the scourge and terror of war for many generations. (Churchill, Roosevelt and Stalin 1943)

The United Nations' own narrative of its history places these events and their commitment to a common goal of peace as precursors to the development of the United Nations as an institution before its official birth in 1945 in San Francisco. These events are framed in terms of a collective agreement to develop a system of international cooperation and, crucially, an emphasis on the responsibility of particular nations to oversee this system's development.

Following these commitments to a new system of international governance, the major powers met at the Dumbarton Oaks Conference in October 1944, at which a blueprint for the structure of the envisaged new world organisation was to be developed in order to be accepted by all nations of the world that were united in their aims for peace (United Nations 2022). The Dumbarton Oaks Conference saw representatives from the United States, the United Kingdom, China and the Soviet Union meet to discuss proposals for the structure of the United Nations. The Dumbarton Oaks proposals, formally known as 'The Washington Conversations on International Peace and Security Organization', contained points on broad aspects of the United Nations, such as its purposes and principles, membership and the principal organs, as well as going into more specific detail about how these organs should function (Dumbarton Oaks 1944). Significantly, this involved a discussion of the role of the Security Council as it was envisaged by those four powerful nations in attendance.

According to the United Nations history books, the essence of the Dumbarton Oaks proposals was that the responsibility for the prevention of war should fall to the Security Council rather than the General Assembly, which was to be made up of five permanent members (the four sponsoring states plus France) and six non-permanent members who would each serve a term of two years (United Nations 2022). The issue of voting within the Security Council was left open to be discussed at a later date, but, otherwise, these proposals were put forward and with extensive media coverage allowing citizens to assess the worth of the plans for ensuring international peace (United Nations 2022). The final pre-San Francisco meeting to discuss the plans for the United Nations was at Yalta in February of 1945. Churchill, Roosevelt and Stalin met to resolve the all-important question of voting within the Security Council and, upon doing so, sent out invitations to the San Francisco conference, which was to begin on 5 March 1945.

With discussions and preparations for the United Nations having occurred in Moscow, Tehran, Washington and Yalta throughout the early 1940s following the Atlantic Charter, forty-six nations were invited to attend the conference in San Francisco, which signified the official birth of the United Nations as an institution. The conference was organised around four commissions representing the four key sections of the planned United Nations Charter, each set to discuss the proposals that were made at Dumbarton Oaks: general purposes, the General Assembly, the Security Council and the International Court of Justice. Unsurprisingly, one of the most contentious points in developing the Charter was the issue of veto power within the Security Council, whereby the permanent members would be able to prevent action agreed upon by the rest of the members. The United Nations alludes to this in their own narrative but states simply:

> One important gap in the Dumbarton Oaks proposals had yet to be filled: the voting procedure in the Security Council. This was done at Yalta in the Crimea where Churchill, Roosevelt and Stalin, together with their foreign ministers and chiefs of staff, met in conference. (United Nations 2022)

Even by its own admission, the United Nations was plagued from the outset by power struggles between the world's most powerful nations and those smaller nations struggling to make their voices count, if they were to be heard at all. However, these issues were seemingly resolved in the vein of working towards a greater good, the Charter was signed by all nations in attendance and the United Nations officially came into existence on 24 October 1945, following the ratification of the Charter by the governments of China, the United Kingdom, the United States, the Soviet Union and France.

ACADEMIC NARRATIVES OF THE UNITED NATIONS

This narrative, to varying degrees, has been replicated and reinforced within historical and political accounts of the development of the United Nations. These accounts show a particular focus on the United Nations as distinct from its chronological predecessor, the League of Nations, and support the idea of the United Nations as a novel institution. Leland Goodrich's account of the history of the United Nations, named simply *The United Nations* (1959), argues that the outbreak of the Second World War indicated the failure of the League of Nations as an international organisation and that no attempt was made to strengthen the League in order to make it more effective, but that instead it was abandoned and replaced with a new structure of global coop-eration (Goodrich 1959). Accounts such as Goodrich's emphasise the novelty of the United Nations as an institution in the same way as the United Nations' history of itself. While the aim of the League of Nations was understood to be an agreement between states to abstain from conflict, the accounts of history we see from Goodrich and others argue that the events of the Second World War 'strengthened the search for a "common law of mankind" under which the rights of the human person, whether individual or in association with his fellows, could be more effectively protected' (Goodwin 1971, 29). This argument follows the line that the unique nature of the events of the Second World War demonstrated that the League of Nations was not equipped to deal with international relations, and as such a new organisation capable of preventing these atrocities needed to be developed. Within these accounts, the Second World War is viewed as the catalyst for the development of a new organisation to deal with international peace and security. This new organisation would represent a fresh start from the League of Nations, allowing the leading governments to distance themselves from its reputation as a failure (Baehr and Gordenker 2005). The events of the Second World War were seen as a clear sign that the existing agreement between particular states in the form of the League of Nations was no longer relevant, and a clean break was required in order to move forward and prevent future wars on this scale. That new organisation had to ensure that the failures of the League of Nations would not be repeated.

The United Nations Conference on International Organization (UNCIO) in San Francisco is often the focal point of these standard accounts of the history of the United Nations. Once they have established the United Nations as a unique organisation, embodying the lessons taught by the perceived failure of the League, these histories turn to San Francisco as its birthplace. The negotiations around what would become the Charter of the United Nations are seen to have taken place in two stages: firstly, through an agreement by the major powers over what were considered to be the main questions and, secondly, through a universal conference of potential member states at San Francisco. The conference at San Francisco, therefore, becomes evidence of the universalism of the United Nations in contrast to the League of Nations in that all potential member states were present for the discussions at San Francisco. In his two-volume book, *A History of the United Nations* (1982), Evan Luard frames San Francisco as a space where for the first time, smaller nations were able to have their say in how this new world organisation would work. Where the League of Nations was selective in its membership, the aim of the United Nations was universal membership, and as such the conference at San Francisco was designed to facilitate discussion between smaller states and the great powers, giving smaller states the opportunity to express their opinions on the draft proposals from Dumbarton Oaks and to influence the content of the Charter (Hurd 2007). This process of negotiation between smaller states and the major powers is reproduced in these standard accounts as an example of how the United Nations dealt with the decline of empire and attempted to create a universal international organisation. These accounts claim that the League of Nations was never truly a global organisation due to the lack of representation for the colonies and that, contrary to this, the United Nations embodied a 'new world order' that would ensure representation for all (Kennedy 2006). However, these accounts do also state that in order for the United Nations to succeed, it was necessary for the world's major powers to take the lead.

The dominance of the sponsoring nations at San Francisco is often viewed as a simple reflection of reality as it was the British, American and Soviet forces that had together defeated the Axis powers and won the Second World War (Archer 1992). However, although this dominance is recognised, it is rarely problematised, due to the perceived universalism of the United Nations. As we saw in the United Nations' own narrative of its development, dominance in the form of the role of the Security Council and the permanent five members was a contentious issue in San Francisco. However, these standard histories argue that the process of discussion and negotiation that took place in San Francisco legitimates this structure, as ultimately the Charter was ratified by all states present (Hurd 2007). The consensus appears to be that the agreement of all states to participate in the United Nations, represented by the signing of the Charter, is sufficient to prove that the dominance of the permanent five members of the Security Council was no longer a problem. Furthermore, the permanent five members are viewed as 'a directorate for governance with narrowly defined emergency powers' (Baehr and Gordenker 2005, 5). Therefore, the dominance of the major powers is not seen as a concern within these histories, as their power was to be limited by the overall universalism of the United Nations and due to the fact that their leadership was supported by all those who signed the Charter at San Francisco.

However, not all of these standard histories are entirely uncritical of the United Nations and its development, particularly with regard to the role of the great powers. While the majority of these accounts argue that the leadership of the sponsoring nations was necessary in order to achieve international cooperation on matters of peace and security, there is also some level of scepticism. Hilderbrand (1990) argues that the United Nations was never thought of as majoritarian in character and that it was understood from the outset that the major powers would have the ultimate authority despite the universalism of the membership. For the United States, the United Nations not only provided an opportunity to take centre stage in an international organisation, but President Roosevelt also used the development of the United Nations as a justification for the US involvement in the Second World War, framing it as a longer-term project of global security (Hilderbrand 1990). The critiques within these standard histories of the United Nations are therefore usually representative of a feeling of scepticism around the intentions of the great powers. Nonetheless, these commonly accepted narratives, both within the United Nations' own account of its history and within academic accounts, are united in certain aspects. These histories, told by academics such as Goodrich (1959) and Goodwin (1971), frame the United Nations as an original response to the horrors of modern existence, and as a democratically evolved structure, embodying principles of global cooperation and international peace. Even where accounts are critical about the dominance of the major powers, they are united with the arguments of Luard (1982) in their acceptance of the United Nations as providing a space for smaller powers to play a role in international peace and security. The universalism of the United Nations as an organisation is legitimised through the framing of the United Nations Conference on International Organisation in San Francisco as a negotiation exercise, and the inclusion of smaller powers is seen as an appropriate response to the decline of the empire.

What is missing from the standard histories of the United Nations outlined here and what will form the basis of the alternative narrative to be explored throughout the following chapters is an account of the role of colonialism. While a number of these standard accounts recognise colonialism as a historical phenomenon, this is only ever acknowledged as something that has been overcome by the development of the United Nations. Within these accounts, the 'problem' of colonialism is solved by the inclusion of former colonies as member states (see Baehr and Gordenker 2005). They suggest that once former colonies have been granted sovereign status and formal independence, colonialism ceases to be an issue. This obscures the fact that the sovereignty granted to former colonies is not equivalent to the sovereignty held by European states. Non-European sovereignty is distinct and inherently vulnerable due to its reliance on the system of international law (Anghie 2005). This approach to colonial power relations that we see within the context of standard histories of the United Nations is therefore insufficient and fails to acknowledge the process by which particular countries came to be great powers while others had to have independence granted to them. It reinforces the ideas that underpin a notion of responsibility within the United Nations – that some states are naturally more advanced and therefore have a duty to lead. Furthermore, former colonies have only succeeded in being granted formal independence through adherence to Western ideas of progress, and their independence was contingent upon their cooperation with newly generated systems of control (Rajagopal 2003). In order to understand the significance of colonialism to the foundations of the United Nations, it is necessary to understand the historical context in which the idea of sovereignty emerges and how this has featured in international institutions.

SOVEREIGNTY AND INTERNATIONAL LAW

International law is framed as a universal system of government as applying
equally to all individuals and all states within the international community
and as being outside of the hierarchy established between states (Orford
2006). However, Anghie (2001) argues that the history of international law
shows it to be explicitly European in origin, and as such we must address the
question of how a system that originated in Europe came to be understood as
universally applicable to all societies in spite of different cultures, beliefs and
political institutions. This acceptance of the universalism of international law
can be attributed to the process of colonialism, by which a European system
of governance came to be a universal system of governance that we now
call international law. Therefore, the argument follows that institutions that
have their basis in international law also have their basis in colonial power
relations.

Based on the principle of the sovereign equality of its members, the United
Nations claims a commitment to the values of international law and settles
disputes in the International Court of Justice accordingly (United Nations
1945). In the preamble, the Charter states that one of the primary aims of the
United Nations is 'to establish conditions under which justice and respect
for the obligations arising from treaties and other sources of international
law can be maintained' (United Nations 1945). However, while the principle
of sovereignty is understood as foundational to international law, it is also
paradoxically a *creation* of international law. The concept of sovereignty did
not precede the development of international law as a system of governing the
behaviour of states towards one another; it is a creation of that very system
(Roth 2011). What is important to understand is how this system comes to
be understood as universal. The United Nations is, by its own admission,
an exercise in cooperation between sovereign states, but this suggests that
sovereignty is an objective status and neglects the history of sovereignty as
a concept. It suggests that sovereignty is equally available to all nations and
means the same when attributed to any individual state. Once we understand
that sovereignty has a colonial history, international institutions with
sovereignty as their foundational principle become much more problematic.

As Anghie (2005) argues, the 'sovereignty doctrine', which forms the basis
of international law, is the result of an attempt to create a legal framework
that could deal with the colonial encounter and the relationship between
Europeans and non-Europeans. Within the colonial context, there was a need
to justify the dominance of one nation over another, and sovereignty was
the way to do this. European colonising empires were deemed sovereign,
while colonial territories were not. International law, therefore, became part
of the civilising mission of colonialism, justifying domination as a means

of teaching the 'uncivilised' world how to be civilised, at which point they would be granted sovereignty (Anghie 2001). Therefore, international law and its potential universality, justified through the concept of sovereignty, was used by Europeans from their position of overwhelming colonial power to feed into the civilizing mission that justified colonialism (Koskenniemi 2005). European domination and power were legitimated through the idea that sovereignty was a universal category that formed the basis of international law, which would be a universal system of governance. Colonialism was framed as the way in which all nations would attain the universal status of sovereignty and hence be able to participate in the international legal system.

This understanding of sovereignty within international law was based on what Anghie (2005) terms the 'dynamic of difference', whereby one culture is framed as universal (and civilised) and the other as particular (and uncivilised), with international law seeking to develop systems to make the particular universal. This process emphasised the difference between two cultures as a difference in levels of civilisation and therefore sought to eradicate difference through the establishment of a universal understanding of what it means to be civilised. By granting sovereignty to European states automatically and suggesting that non-European states must earn their sovereignty, the universalisation of international law was not simply an impartial inclusion of all the world's people into an objective system of governance but rather made it necessary for all nations to conform to a particular form of social and political organisation in order to participate in the international community (Pahuja 2011). As international law was historically, conceptually and inherently European, non-European nations had to conform to European forms of organisation in order to participate and be understood as civilised.

By making sovereignty foundational to international law and framing international law as universally applicable, but only allowing European states to be deemed sovereign in the first instance, it was possible to create a system in which states outside of Europe were regarded as existing in an earlier stage of development. The cultural characteristics of sovereignty then become the cultural characteristics of Europe, and thus Europe is equated with civilisation, whereas non-Europeans are considered culturally and politically 'immature' (Grovogui 1996). The significance of this within the context of international institutions, firstly in the League of Nations and later in the United Nations, is that European dominance, particularly through schemes such as the mandate system or the trusteeship system, was legitimised through linear understandings of progress and civilisation. Colonies were not only simply encouraged to be European but also encouraged to be *civilised* to participate in global interactions. These systems were justified as assisting colonised peoples to attain sovereign status within the framework of international law, legitimising colonial rule through the concept of development (Rajagopal 2003). Within this framework, colonialism can only be viewed as a positive attempt to assist less-developed nations to become civilised and able to participate in a global network. Colonial violence, domination and the eradication of cultural difference are framed as a generous act of support or education.

However, even in attaining sovereign status, the sovereignty granted to non-Europeans was distinct. While European nations were deemed sovereign from the outset within the system of international law due to their ability to participate as a result of their advanced level of social complexity and enlightenment, non-European nations had to be granted sovereignty. Thus, in developing the concept of sovereignty, international law and its associated institutions created two different models: European sovereignty, which was automatic due to the advanced civilisation of European societies, and non-European sovereignty, which could be granted once those societies had followed European paths of development. The discourse of development that had been created in order to justify colonialism is fed into the establishment of a system of international law, whereby non-European sovereignty is understood as a specific stage of development for those deemed not yet ready for full sovereignty as a consequence of their 'primitive' culture (Grovogui 1996). This notion of development meant that while international law and the international community more broadly were considered universal, Europe would always remain the prime example of what it meant to be civilised, and as a result substantive equality between sovereigns could be prevented (Pahuja 2011). The colonies then could participate in international law as sovereign states once those states that already held sovereign status deemed them ready, but the sovereignty granted to them would never be equivalent. This meant that prior to the Second World War, international law was only applicable to sovereign (i.e. European) states, and as a result virtually no conduct towards Asian and African states could be questioned (Anand 2010).

As with most aspects of social organisation that we consider constitutive of modernity, the conventional narrative of international law is that it developed in Europe and was spread out to the rest of the world until it was universal. This universalism suggests a level of inclusivity, allowing international law to disguise its colonial origins and actually appear anti-colonial (Pahuja 2011). While colonialism is associated with dominance and inequality, the perceived universality of international law implies equality between all nations under one single system of governance, concealing its intricate relationship with colonialism. This established Eurocentric narrative of international law hides the way in which Western culture was forcefully implemented through the process of colonisation (Fassbender and Peters 2012). Even where colonialism is recognised as significant in the development of international law within conventional narratives, the assumption is that colonial domination ended with formal decolonisation. However, this disguises the way in which sovereignty developed as a concept within international law and how it was designed to ensure the continued dominance of European culture (Anghie 2014). Colonialism did not end with decolonisation because international law and the concept of sovereignty play a key role in perpetuating the inequalities that characterised formal colonialism. Ideas of civilisation and difference still feature heavily in debates around sovereignty in spite of common understandings that we now live in a postcolonial world. Due to its history, the concept of sovereignty continues to enable certain political structures, such as those based on fixed territory, and disables others, such as those based on solidarities across territorial borders (Jones 2013). The notion of sovereignty, therefore, plays a key role in maintaining the existing hierarchical order in world politics and does so through its ability to disguise its colonial origins and present itself as universal and objective.

SOVEREIGNTY AND THE LEAGUE OF NATIONS

Like the United Nations after it, the League of Nations signified the cooperation of independent states, which ultimately rested on the belief in the sovereignty of each individual state. While the League of Nations was a collective, it was not designed to diminish the right of each individual state to rule over its own territories. Sovereignty in this context is therefore understood in terms of what Moses (2014) calls 'de facto sovereignty', which refers to an understanding of sovereignty as the right of states to make final decisions regarding their territories and not to be governed by the rules of other states within international organisations. The League of Nations represented an agreement that states would cooperate in order to attempt to prevent another world war, but individual states ultimately retained the power to make their own decisions, not being held accountable to the rules of behaviour that governed other states. Rather than creating a world government, the League of Nations signified an agreement between individual states to respect the sovereignty of one another and to not act aggressively towards one another. In line with this, it was generally agreed that each national government should retain control over its military forces. Despite Article 8 of the Covenant requesting that national armaments be reduced to 'the lowest point consistent with national safety' and a requirement that members exchange 'full and frank information as to the scale of their armaments', these military forces remained under national control (League of Nations 1919). There was no obligation for states to surrender their military forces and any decision to participate in collective military action remained the decision of the individual state. Sovereignty in this context then was the right of each nation to maintain control, both in terms of their military forces and their ability to make their own decisions regarding responses to acts of aggression and international conflict. However, sovereignty was also a key concern in relation to colonial territories and those territories liberated from the defeated powers of the First World War.

The League of Nations established the mandate system in order to manage those territories that had belonged to the defeated parties of the First World War. The aim of this system was, in theory, to provide some level of accountability on the part of the victorious powers so that the mandated territories were not simply subsumed into existing empires, with critics of colonialism insisting that European powers acted as 'colonialists with a conscience' (Grovogui 1996, 112). In principle, mandatory administration was intended to make the imperial rule a project of development in order to prepare territories for self-government; however, in reality, perhaps unsurprisingly, it failed to do so (Pedersen 2015). The concept of sovereignty was key to the League's approach to mandated territories and caused a significant level of dispute between its members. The mandate system claimed to be acting to prevent conquering powers from gaining full sovereignty and hence full control of the mandated territory and its military forces, but it was not made clear to whom this sovereignty belonged either in the Covenant or in later discussions. The mandated territories were certainly not considered sovereign themselves, but neither could the League be seen to be transferring territories from the hands of one imperial master to another. The result was that neither the mandated territory nor the mandatory power was considered to have sovereignty over the territory, and as such sovereignty was simply absent from these spaces altogether (Pedersen 2015).

However, in the absence of sovereignty being granted to the mandatory power, sovereignty could not be denied to these territories forever. What the mandate system attempted to establish was that these territories were working towards self-government, with Article 22 of the Covenant referring to 'peoples not yet able to stand by themselves' (League of Nations 1919). In theory, the mandated territory would be recognised as sovereign and cease to be governed by an imperial power directly and the League of Nations indirectly once it was considered 'civilised'. In reality, the mandatory power decided the moment at which the mandated territory had achieved a sufficient level of civilisation that independence was appropriate (Grant 2007). Although the mandate system claimed to be a process of granting sovereignty to the territories that had formerly belonged to the empires of the defeated parties of the First World War, in actuality, it formed part of a process of imperial legitimation. By granting imperial powers the responsibility of overseeing the development of these territories into civilised sovereign states, the mandate system justified imperial rule as a system of domination. It allowed the sovereignty of colonial territories to be determined by imperial powers.

The mandate system reinforced those ideas about development and civilisation that justified the colonial project via Eurocentric conceptions of modernity. By understanding colonial territories as existing in an earlier stage of development than imperial powers, it was possible to justify both colonialism and the mandate system as projects of tutelage, with colonisation acting as the means to political, economic and social development (Grovogui 1996). The League of Nations embraced the already established colonial discourse of civilisation that allowed countries to be ranked in terms of their adherence to European cultural values, defining the mandate system as a relationship between the civilised and the uncivilised (Grant 2007). Cultural difference within the mandate system was therefore viewed as a distinction between 'backwards' and 'advanced' nations, with those nations categorised as advanced bearing the responsibility to teach the people of 'backwards' territories how to advance (Anghie 2001). The League of Nations, through the mandate system, reinforced those problematic ideas about difference and civilisation that justified the colonial project from its outset and created a dynamic of selective responsibility whereby European powers via the League of Nations were responsible – in principle – for supporting 'development' in colonial territories, but without any significant monitoring. Administering powers could utilise the concept of responsibility to justify their presence within colonial states, but in reality the mandate system amounted to the institutionalisation of exploitation (Grovogui 1996).

As Anghie (2001) argues, the significance of sovereignty within this framework has two key aspects. Firstly, sovereignty became the promised reward for territories that exhibited desirable behaviour, and the mandate system encouraged this with the support of the discourse of civilisation. The mandate system was presented as a process of development that would allow those territories that were not deemed ready for self-government to be supervised by nations at the height of civilisation in order that the whole world would be a better place. As such, sovereignty was used as the ultimate reward for territories that showed their ability to be a part of a global civilised society through adherence to European cultural values. Secondly, however, Anghie (2001) argues that the sovereignty that would be granted to non-European territories within the League of Nations framework was distinctive by virtue of it having to be granted, rather than being inherent as it was for European nations; this system established European sovereignty and non-European sovereignty as two distinct categories. Therefore, the mandate system used the concept of sovereignty as an incentive for the people of mandated territories to behave in particular ways, without acknowledging that the sovereignty that would be granted to them would never be equivalent to the sovereignty held by European nations. The fact that the imperial authorities had the power to decide when mandates had reached the point at which sovereignty could or should be granted clearly shows that the right to govern associated with mandates and mandatory powers was distinct. The significance of the idea of sovereignty within the League of Nations, therefore, is that it enabled the development of new systems of control that were informed by imperial discourse.

The elasticity of sovereignty within the League of Nations is also seen clearly in its decisions around membership. In principle, the League represented an organisation of sovereign states, and so logically states were either sovereign and therefore eligible to join or not sovereign and unable to join. However, in considering the membership of smaller European states such as Latvia, Estonia and Lithuania, the League proposed modified terms of membership such as restricted voting rights and representation via larger European states (Getachew 2019). Equally, Ethiopia and Liberia were given qualified membership that saw them subject to a 'system of oversight' designed to 'civilize' these states on the basis of an insistence that they continued to practice slavery (Getachew 2019). These two examples demonstrate that while sovereignty was a vital principle for the League of Nations, it was not a fixed status that states either had or did not have. Rather, it could be conditional and hierarchical.

For those states at the top of the hierarchy, sovereignty formed the basis of the relationship between them in terms of their right to make final decisions and rule their territories. Sovereignty in this context represented the idea that despite the League of Nations signifying an agreement to engage in collective security, members retained ultimate authority over their level of involvement and collective security amounted to a commitment to respect the sovereignty of other states by resisting acts of military aggression. The principle of 'domestic jurisdiction' was of particular significance for the original signatories of the Covenant, meaning that states retained freedom of action and the international community via the League of Nations would not intervene in matters that were considered 'domestic affairs' (Glanville 2013). The League of Nations was not to be an organisation that told member states what they could and could not do within their own territories. This commitment to non-intervention in the domestic affairs of states was seen in the rejection of requests for equality to be written into the Covenant, such as the Japanese proposals for racial equality (Glanville 2013). The desire to maintain national sovereignty, meaning the right of states to govern within their own territories – colonies included – was therefore fundamental for those states signing the Covenant of the League of Nations, which was the first real attempt at international cooperation of states as opposed to individual partnerships between states.

However, the outbreak of the Second World War resulted in the League of Nations being deemed a failure and calls for a new way to deal with an increasingly global world. The notion of sovereignty and respect for the sovereignty of individual states that had been written into the League of Nations was no longer considered sufficient in dealing with potential acts of aggression by the major military powers and so a new way of organising the world was required (MacQueen 2011). Keen to distance itself from the negativity surrounding the imperialism of the League, the United Nations began discussing international relations not in terms of sovereignty but in terms of sovereign *equality* instead.

FROM SOVEREIGNTY TO SOVEREIGN EQUALITY

As noted earlier in the chapter, the United Nations sought to frame itself as a new organisation aiming to address the failures of the League of Nations, which had been universally proclaimed a failure. As a significant amount of criticism had been levelled at the League for being exclusive and protecting the rights of individual states too much, the United Nations sought to promote itself as a universal institution with the potential for global membership. In doing so, it had to appear inclusive and committed to equality and equal representation. Where the League had been criticised for its respect for the national sovereignty of its exclusive members, the United Nations began with a commitment to *equality* in terms of the sovereignty of its much broader membership (MacQueen 2011). However, the rhetoric of sovereign equality that we see in the formation of the United Nations still fails to acknowledge the colonial origins of the concept of sovereignty itself. Furthermore, the privileging of the sovereignty of certain nations over and above that of other nations as well as the United Nations' continuation of the power structures established by the League render claims to 'equality' both problematic and misleading.

In contrast to the League of Nations, the United Nations wished to avoid the sense of inefficiency in decision-making associated with the protection of national sovereignty and the control retained by individual governments. Instead, it was promoted as allowing for effective collective action where required, while retaining the 'purity' of national sovereignty (Schlesinger 2003). Governments would still be considered sovereign, but with a greater sense of international responsibility attached to this sovereignty within the United Nations. The aim was to create an institution that could deal with problems of international conflict and security through collective decision-making, rather than leaving decisions around intervention and military aggression at the hands of individual governments, as had been seen in the

League. In order to address this, the focus of the United Nations became less an issue of protecting national sovereignty and more an issue of promoting and respecting sovereign *equality*. While this pledge to sovereign equality might appear on the surface as a commitment to addressing power within the international system, Krasner (2009) argues that both Westphalian sovereignty and international legal sovereignty are best understood through the concept of 'organized hypocrisy'. Asymmetries of power and the absence of clear mechanisms for resolving conflicts between states mean that governments will not always adhere to the rules and norms of the international arena if the consequences of violating these rules offer a material or ideological incentive to do so (Krasner 2009). States might agree to a system that respects the sovereignty and agrees that sovereign states are equal, but the reality is that states will often deviate from the norms of such a system in order to serve their own interests. These contradictions and hypocrisies were clear in the organisation of the League of Nations and remain in the organisation of the United Nations, despite its claims otherwise.

The preamble to the Charter is the first reference to equality within the United Nations, affirming 'the equal rights of all men and women and of nations large and small' (United Nations 1945, 2). This definition was much the same within the context of the League of Nations, but as the Charter progressed, the significant difference was the focus not just on sovereignty but on sovereign equality. Article 2 of the Charter asserts this explicitly, stating that 'the Organization is based on the principle of the sovereign equality of all its Members' and also emphasises the obligations of the Charter as applicable to 'all members' (United Nations 1945, 3). The United Nations was in much the same way as its predecessor, a cooperative body of independently existing sovereign states; however, their fundamental equality was, in this case, explicitly stipulated in the language of the governing documents, where it had been rather more implicit in the League of Nations. It would seem then, that the United Nations was trying in theory to avoid affording individual governments the power to dominate international relations. However, it becomes difficult not to be sceptical of these claims once the structure of the organisation is examined in more detail, and it seems that the initial claims to equality are actually present in order to disguise the incredibly unequal power relations built into the institution.

Patil (2008) argues that the Charter of the United Nations is ultimately an expression of the sovereignty of the Western powers, formalising their rights as sovereign nations over the rights of colonies and dependent territories, which are not included in this claim to equality as a result of not being considered sovereign. The emphasis of the Charter is not on equality per se. However, sovereign equality works to exclude those territories and peoples not yet considered sovereign by the international community, that is, existing colonies and territories held under the League of Nations mandate system, which would soon transform into the trusteeship system of the United Nations. As such, the claims to equality made in the Charter are somewhat misleading as they only apply to those nations already considered sovereign. This creates a hierarchy within the international community whereby the rights of existing sovereign (imperial) states are enshrined in the Charter as a fundamental principle, making the prospect of decolonisation problematic (Patil 2008). The sovereignty of the initial member states of the United Nations is written into the Charter as its primary principle, meaning that the rights of colonies and other non-self-governing territories will always be secondary to the right of sovereign states to govern those territories, and this framework is clearly a problematic starting point for the process of decolonisation.

The United Nations is frequently praised for leading colonies to independence, with Baehr and Gordenker stating that 'most of the present UN members are former colonies that gained political independence through direct or indirect involvement with the United Nations' (2005, 114). While it is undeniable that decolonisation gained momentum following the establishment of the United Nations, to attribute this to the United Nations itself is deceptive and silences the intense work of the anti-colonial movement in pushing for decolonisation, which forms the basis of the chapters that will follow. However, for the purposes of the discussion here, the more significant point is that although a large number of countries have gained independence since 1945, the sovereignty that is granted to them is not equal to the sovereignty of the initial member states of the United Nations. The sovereignty granted to former colonies and dependent territories through decolonisation via the United Nations would never be equivalent to the inherent sovereignty of Western nations that were enshrined in the principles of the Charter. The very fact that one form of sovereignty is natural and the other must be granted – based on adherence to European ideas of civilisation – surely makes the idea of sovereign equality for these nations impossible.

As Pahuja (2011) argues, the discourse of development does the work of reconciling the contradictions between the commitment to sovereign equality and the fact that certain nations remain under imperial control, allowing the United Nations to exist as an institution committed to universality while also emphasising Western values as exemplary. The standard narrative of development and progress allows the idea of sovereign equality to exist without meaning actual equality for all nations through the categorisation of colonies and dependent territories as existing in an earlier stage of development and by holding sovereignty and sovereign equality as the ultimate end goal. This is an example of what Bhabha (1994) calls a 'time-lag' of cultural difference, whereby nations that do not conform to European cultural values are framed as existing in an earlier period of history, while always being on the path of progress. However, this narrative of development fails to recognise that the sovereignty granted through decolonisation is in a secondary form, not equivalent. No matter how long these former colonies travel on the road to progress, they will never reach the prize of sovereignty that is equivalent to the sovereignty inherently characteristic of their imperial masters.

To view sovereign equality within the United Nations in the way suggested here reiterates the colonial foundations of the concept of sovereignty, whereby sovereignty is used to legitimate a global hierarchy of power. The concept itself is intrinsically colonial, as its initial function was to justify the imperial rule. To continue to use the concept of sovereignty as a way of understanding the place of different territories within the international community is, therefore, a form of postcolonial power. In spite of formal decolonisation, the idea of sovereignty is bound up in its colonial history and can never be a neutral status, nor can it ever apply to all territories equally. An international system of governance based on the sovereignty of states will always be a European system of governance (Archer 1992). The fact that the United Nations emphasised sovereignty as the primary principle of relations between states is evidence that it was not a revolutionary institution, and in spite of the decolonisation seen since 1945, the United Nations is ultimately a product of empire (Mazower 2009).

SOVEREIGN EQUALITY AND TRUSTEESHIP

In addition to the ways in which the concept of sovereignty itself can be criticised from the perspective of its colonial origins, the United Nations' formal commitment to sovereign equality is undermined when we examine the systems designed to deal with the management of colonial territories and how they were developed. These systems can be understood as neocolonial technologies of power, which are strategies of control designed to replace colonial practices as the key instruments of imperialism in the face of decolonisation and independence (Nkrumah 1965). The trusteeship system of the United Nations was little more than a rebranding of the League of Nations mandate system and, as such, saw the continuation of associated forms of colonial power and domination. The trusteeship system signifies yet another way in which the United Nations was the product of evolution from the League, not a revolutionary approach to international politics (Mazower 2009).

As detailed earlier in the chapter, Article 22 of the Covenant of the League of Nations established former colonial possessions of the defeated parties of the First World War as mandate territories to be supervised by imperial powers. These territories were categorised based on the degree to which they were deemed 'able to stand by themselves' (League of Nations 1919). As has also been previously highlighted, many of the ideologies and structures present in the League of Nations were modified and rebranded for their inclusion in the United Nations. The dissolution of the League of Nations meant the end of the mandate system and thus an opening for a different approach to negotiating the colonial relationship. However, even in the face of public pressure around decolonisation, the United Nations did little to encourage independence for those territories that had been subject to subordination by the mandate system (Sherwood 1996). Rather, they were to be transferred to a rebranded mandate system in the form of the United Nations' trusteeship system, with Article 77 of the Charter of the United Nations detailing the territories that should be dealt with under this new system. Article 77 of the Charter reads as follows:

1. The trusteeship system shall apply to such territories in the following categories as may be placed thereunder by means of trusteeship agreements:

   a. territories now held under mandate;
   b. territories which may be detached from enemy states as a result of the Second World War; and
   c. territories voluntarily placed under the system by states responsible for their administration. (United Nations 1945)

Despite the grand claims to equality outlined in the preamble of the Charter, the United Nations failed to establish decolonisation and independence for the colonies as reasonable objectives for the international community. This new system saw a continuation of the colonial relationships supported by the mandate system in the League of Nations. Indeed, Article 79 of the Charter states that:

The terms of trusteeship for each territory to be placed under the trusteeship system, including any alteration or amendment, shall be agreed upon by the states directly concerned, including the mandatory power in the case of territories held under mandate by a Member of the United Nations. (United Nations 1945)

The trusteeship system established by the United Nations did not seek to transfer control from imperial powers to an international organisation in order to begin the process of decolonisation. Rather, it sought to establish a system that appeared to be beginning this process while maintaining the rights of colonisers to rule their territories as they saw fit. The system of trusteeship established by the United Nations continued the colonial ideologies established in the League with a focus on development and progress with Western liberalism as the ultimate goal for all states (Getachew 2019). The trusteeship system reinforced colonial ideologies whereby Europe was equated with development. However, the existence of neocolonial relationships established through the system of trusteeship in the context of the rhetoric around equality in the United Nations is clearly contradictory.

Although the sponsoring nations wished to frame the United Nations as a new organisation that would succeed where the League of Nations had failed, the issue of colonialism and colonial independence did not appear to feature as a high priority. Concerns around national sovereignty were with regards to relationships between colonial powers themselves as opposed to relationships between colonial powers and their colonies or dependent territories. Indeed, the motivational forces that had led to the development of the League after the First World War were, to a large extent, the same motivations that prompted the development of the United Nations, that is, a system of international cooperation to prevent wars between powerful states (Haas 2009). The relationships between these powerful states and their colonies were not seen to be within the scope of international organisations, as to challenge colonialism was to challenge the sovereignty of imperial powers. Although the rhetoric of the United Nations suggests that its establishment was a response to the events of the Second World War, creating an organisation capable of protecting *individuals* from the violence such as the Second World War had seen, in reality, it was filling the space left by the League in terms of a formal agreement between powerful states to avoid conflict on a global scale. The trusteeship system was developed in the process of the establishment of the United Nations to manage the colonial territories that had formerly belonged to the League of Nations mandate system and those that had been taken from the defeated parties of the Second World War while recognising that the mandate system could not be continued under the same name.

The system of trusteeship outlined in the Charter of the United Nations perpetuates the notions of development and civilisation present in the mandate system of the League of Nations, ensuring that imperial powers have control over the development of particular nations in order for them to be granted independence and to be recognised as sovereign states (Rajagopal 2003). As with the mandate system, the principle of trusteeship was based upon a narrative that distinguished between developed, wise and paternalistic administrating authorities (i.e. imperial powers) and undeveloped, irrational and childlike dependent territories to justify a system of control and domination (Patil 2008). This narrative of development and the potential for eventual self-government legitimated the trusteeship system. While this system appears to be addressing the increasingly contentious issue of decolonisation on the basis that dependent territories will be guided to independence via trusteeship, the rhetoric of sovereign equality that features so heavily in the United Nations' founding documents disguises its neocolonial mechanisms of control. The idea of tutelage reinforces a world view with Europe as the height of civilisation and other cultures as existing in an earlier stage of progress.

The trusteeship system that was formed by the United Nations was not, therefore, a system that would recognise the sovereignty of all states in line with a commitment to sovereign equality. Rather, the notion of sovereign equality stood in contradiction to the trusteeship system, which allowed for the continuation of the colonial management of colonies and dependent territories. The trusteeship system reinforced problematic ideologies of development that supported a hierarchy in terms of civilisation, recognising the inherent sovereignty and equality of developed Western states and the need for other parts of the world to earn their sovereignty through adherence to Western values. Chapters 2 and 3 explore these issues in more detail, particularly in identifying the international actors who played a key role in developing both the mandate system and trusteeship.

A COLONIAL HISTORY OF THE UNITED NATIONS

To be explicit, the argument of this chapter is that in contrast to the standard histories that present it as a novel institution, the United Nations was, in fact, 'the product of evolution, not revolution' (Mazower 2009, 17). Where the birth of the United Nations is usually presented as a particular moment in history and as the dawn of a new era in an international organisation, this chapter has shown that the United Nations has a much stronger basis in the League of Nations than is usually acknowledged. In order to understand the impact of colonial power relations on the contemporary relationships between the most and least powerful nations of the world, it is necessary to reconsider the history of the United Nations and to disturb the dominant discourses of equality upon which the organisation is based through taking into account the relationship between the two institutions. The League of Nations is often cited as the predecessor to the United Nations chronologically, but as we have seen in the examination of the standard historical narrative, there is a strong desire to view the United Nations as a clean break and as a new, more inclusive organisation. There is an attempt to view the Second World War as a rupture in international politics that signalled the need for an entirely new approach to governing the relationships between states and a new form of an international organisation that would prevent war and maintain security. However, if we reject this narrative of rupture and see the United Nations not as a unique institution but as a rebranding and continuation of the League of

Nations, the colonial history it wished to forget becomes much more apparent. This chapter has been the initial presentation of an alternative historical narrative that will be developed throughout the following chapters. Suppose we understand the ways in which the League of Nations was inherently colonial and reject the narrative of the United Nations as an original institution. In that case, we can fully understand the perpetuation of colonial power structures in the contemporary international context. It allows us to appreciate the colonial discourses of civilisation, development and progress that underpin a framing of the West as responsible for maintaining international security.

Despite the League's written intention to develop a system capable of maintaining international peace and security, it proved to be relatively ineffective, as 1939 saw the outbreak of the Second World War and calls for the need for a more effective way of dealing with international conflict, which is where discussions around the United Nations pick up. In reality, the failure of the League of Nations was partly the result of an absence of involvement on the part of two key governments – the United States and the Soviet Union – and the success of any following international institutions would be reliant upon their involvement, which required some degree of rebranding (Hilderbrand 1990).

The concurrent timing of the development of the United Nations with the United States' involvement in the Second World War meant that President Roosevelt was able to use the United Nations to justify American involvement in the war by constructing its ultimate purpose as something longer term (Hilderbrand 1990). If the United States could be seen as participating in a global organisation to prevent breaches to the peace, their involvement in the Second World War as part of this process could be justified. Thus, the disassociation between the League of Nations and the United Nations was less a case of difference in objectives; after all, both organisations had international peace and security as their primary purpose, and more a case of political PR. The aim was to create an organisation capable of dealing with international relations on a global scale, but this time, with the support of the United States and the Soviet Union. Leaders were able to disconnect the United Nations from its predecessor by framing its development as a response to the Second World War, supporting enlightenment ideas of universalism and progress, as signifying a new world order, rather than as a continuation of existing global power relations. The rising power and influence of the United States at this time, therefore, made their involvement essential.

This approach to understanding the history of the United Nations highlights the relationship between the United Nations and the League of Nations, indicating the inaccuracies of the standard narrative of rupture between the two organisations that allow for a dominant discourse of equality to be associated with the United Nations. If, instead, we understand the United

Nations as the product of a PR campaign to protect the relationships between the major powers of the League, but also to create an organisation that included the rising powers of the time, we are able to disturb these dominant discourses. This reconsideration of the history of the United Nations provides a base from which we can understand the relationship between the United Nations and colonialism, showing the extent to which colonial power structures that enable selective responsibility in the present were built into the organisation from the very beginning.

This chapter has provided the context for the alternative historical narrative that follows in the remaining chapters of the book. It has established both the historiographical intervention being made and some of the core theoretical critiques in relation to the concept of sovereignty that underpins international governance. While the standard narratives of the United Nations' development emphasise novelty and a commitment to equality, the chapters that follow will explore an alternative narrative that is centred around the continuation of colonial power structures and a long history of resistance.

Chapter 2

Resistance to Imperialism and the Two Leagues

The League of Nations was established following the Paris Peace Conference of 1919, amid talk of internationalism and universalism that provided a glimmer of hope for anti-colonial movements and those living under colonial rule. However, it became clear rather rapidly that the brotherhood proposed by those present in Paris would not extend beyond European borders. This chapter looks in more detail at the mandate system of the League of Nations and the issue of sovereignty introduced in the previous chapter in providing the context for the development of the League against Imperialism. The League against Imperialism was established in 1927 to unify the anti-colonial anger felt by many across the globe into a formal organisation working towards an alternative vision of internationalism and in response to the unfulfilled promises made at the Paris Peace Conference. Using archival material from the League against Imperialism itself, this chapter provides an original and evidenced critique of the concepts of universalism and internationalism advocated by those powers within the League of Nations that simultaneously sustained direct and indirect forms of colonial domination. The League against Imperialism was a significant moment in anti-colonial resistance and often neglected in accounts of international organisations, although it has received more attention in recent years (see, for example, Louro 2018; Petersson 2014).

In order that we might more accurately understand the extent to which colonial power structures have been built into international institutions, it is necessary to challenge accepted narratives through the provision of alternative, evidenced narratives. Building on the arguments laid out in chapter 1, this chapter examines the League of Nations as the precursor to the United Nations, re-narrating its history to account for the resistance movements that challenged its power. The purpose of doing so is twofold: firstly, to

demonstrate the centrality of colonial power dynamics to international institutions that make claims to equality and the foundational principle of sovereignty; and secondly, to emphasise the extent to which the institutionalisation
of these power dynamics was challenged *at the time*, rather than this being a
later reflection on how the organisation functioned.

PRESIDENT WILSON AND THE
PARIS PEACE CONFERENCE

The Paris Peace Conference began on 18 January 1919, and resulted in the
well-known Treaty of Versailles and the site at which the League of Nations
was established. Following the conclusion of the First World War in 1918,
the Paris Peace Conference was not only a meeting where the allied powers
could decide upon consequences for defeated states and redistribute their
colonial territories but also a space for the allied powers to develop a system
for maintaining international peace that would prevent the outbreak of further
war. The war had highlighted the unambiguous failure of traditional methods
of peacekeeping, which had relied on agreements between individual states,
and the need for an alternative approach (Birn 1981). Therefore, the Paris
Peace Conference was not only the stage for a peace treaty to end the war but
also the place at which a new world order was being imagined. As Margaret
Macmillan (2003) recounts in *Paris 1919: Six Months That Changed the
World,* the Peace Conference saw representatives from all over the world
congregate in Paris greeted by petitions on a range of issues from women's
suffrage to disarmament to workers' rights. The rarity of such a concentration
of political power drew attention from across the globe, and citizens saw this
as an opportunity to push the major powers into imagining a different kind
of world on many different fronts of inequality. For a vast number of hopeful
existing and former colonies, the Paris Peace Conference appeared on paper
to be an opportunity for democracy and freedom to prevail, particularly in
light of statements made by the United States.

During the First World War, US president Woodrow Wilson had become
a vocal advocate for the principles of democracy, collective security and
self-determination (Steel 1998). For this chapter, examining Wilson's
approach provides some important context to the development of anti-
colonial movements after the establishment of the League of Nations. In
his public statements, President Wilson frequently projected a vision for
an international institution that would ensure peace, and prior to the Paris
Peace Conference, he put forward a Fourteen Point proposal that reflected
this vision (Wilson 1918). Much has been made of this 'Wilsonian' moment
in international relations, and Manela (2007) has highlighted the particular

significance of Wilson's ideals for colonised peoples, who saw his argument for government rule by popular consent as a direct challenge to imperialism. In the minds of the colonised, Wilson's solution for world peace was liberalism that provided no space for continued European domination, and thus, any international body grounded in the principle of self-determination and consent of the governed would necessarily put an end to colonialism. As this chapter will demonstrate, Wilson's vision was, in fact, much less radical. However nonetheless, it signifies an important moment in international relations where the West was forced to reckon with the paradox of a commitment to self-determination and continuation of imperialism.

In providing a solution to the problem of war, Wilson's Fourteen Points proposal begins by arguing that the time has passed for 'secret covenants' and that a new world must be imagined:

> It is that the world be made fit and safe to live in; and particularly that it be made safe for every peace-loving nation which, like our own, wishes to live its own life, determine its own institutions, be assured of justice and fair dealing by the other peoples of the world as against force and selfish aggression. (Wilson 1918)

It is not difficult to see why Wilson's approach resonated with those fighting for independence. Talk of peace, justice and the ability to determine their institutions led the colonised to believe that Wilson was in support of decolonisation. If this opening paragraph had not been sufficiently explicit in its aims, point five of Wilson's plan stated the need for

> a free, open-minded, and absolutely impartial adjustment of all colonial claims, based upon a strict observance of the principle that in determining all such questions of sovereignty the interests of the populations concerned must have equal weight with the equitable claims of the government whose title is to be determined. (Wilson 1918)

For former and existing colonies, this commitment to self-determination and an impartial assessment of colonial claims that would take into account the interests of the populations concerned looked remarkably like support for decolonisation movements and independence. In outlining his plans for an international assembly of nations, Wilson came to be seen as a champion for the principles of sovereignty, democracy and self-government, reflecting consideration of the interests of colonial populations in comparison to a distinct lack of such consideration on the part of the imperial powers. Those who had been working tirelessly to realise independence for the colonies had hoped

Wilson's vision would provide the catalyst for decolonisation and the start of an equal distribution of power internationally.

This concept of self-determination became central to Wilson's rhetoric around establishing a new world order but was nonetheless relatively ill-defined. In a manner that will become repetitive throughout this book in the recounting of statements made by major powers, Wilson's idea of self-determination was both unclear in terms of its actual meaning and seemingly applied only selectively. Was Wilson promoting independence and self-government for all of the colonies? His statement suggested that colonial populations should have a say in determining questions of sovereignty, but how this was to be balanced in 'equal weight' with the claims of existing governing powers was not clear. In Paris, there was much confusion among commentators over what Wilson meant by the term 'self-determination' and whether it required self-government, involvement or a voice in government or national independence. This lack of clarity was further exacerbated by Wilson's public position on the specific question of Irish independence, which he believed to be a domestic matter for Britain to decide (Macmillan 2003). Nevertheless, hearing the president of the United States talk about the need for self-determination provided a beacon of hope for those living under colonial rule.

By the time the Peace Conference concluded in 1920, it had become clear that Wilson had neither the power nor the desire to be a representative of colonial interests. Despite pleas from India for Wilson to push for decolonisation as a key feature in the design of a new international institution, he was unwilling to represent demands that conflicted with the interests of the major powers, particularly France and Britain (Manela 2006). For Wilson, it seemed that the Paris Conference was not the correct forum within which to challenge the imperial domination of the Allied powers, with him believing instead that these issues would inevitably be resolved by the establishment of the League of Nations (Manela 2006). This proved disappointing for those pushing for decolonisation, representing a missed opportunity on the part of the United States and fuelling an even more intense desire to continue to challenge imperial power.

THE LEAGUE OF NATIONS, SELF-DETERMINATION AND THE MANDATE SYSTEM

These debates around self-determination and the governing of colonial territories continued throughout the conference in Paris. A broader look at the principles enshrined in the founding documents of the League draws attention to the contradictions and conflicts between claims around self-determination and the perpetuation of imperialism, and an examination of the mandate system makes clear the problematic discourses that underpin these contradictions, allowing for the development of an international system grounded in inequality. The Covenant of the League of Nations was signed on 28 June 1919, and signified a commitment by the largely European founding members of the League of Nations to attempt to put an end to the 'international anarchy' that had been the result of traditional approaches to peacekeeping (Birn 1981, 6). The outbreak of the First World War in 1914 suggested that previously existing diplomatic strategies were ineffective for dealing with global affairs and that an international union of nations would be necessary to prevent future conflicts. The founding members of the League of Nations argued that this permanent coalition of states would bring about the abolition of war on a global scale and that, as a result, international relations would be significantly less hostile.

With this objective in mind, the Covenant itself states that signing parties agree to:

> Obligations not to resort to war . . . open, just and honourable relations between nations . . . the firm establishment of the understandings of international law as the actual rule of conduct among Governments . . . respect for all treaty obligations in the dealings of organised peoples with one another. (League of Nations 1919)

These foundational principles upon which the League was based were designed 'in order to promote international co-operation and to achieve international peace and security' (League of Nations 1919). The language used in the first section of this governing document sets out ideals of international cooperation in promoting peaceful relations, but with a solid foundation in international law as the basis for relationships between states. It also frames peaceful relations between nations as an 'obligation', that is, as a duty or responsibility of 'organised peoples', rather than as a choice for states in their dealings with others. Given the concurrent continuation of imperial power, we might infer here which nations were being imagined when the Covenant refers to 'organised peoples' and which nations would not be included in these open, just and honourable relations.

This approach also explains the paradox of Wilson's commitment to self-determination alongside his acceptance of imperialism. For the major powers, self-determination as independence of self-government could only apply to 'organised peoples', and as will become apparent in this section, those living under colonial rule were not considered such. Wilson, alongside South African statesman Jan Smuts, 'recast self-determination in the service of empire' (Getachew 2019, 40). They took the concept of self-determination and used it in ways that would maintain colonial and racial hierarchies.

Paradoxically, self-determination was presented as a universal principle while arguing that it did not apply to the colonies, which required tutelage and discipline via empire in order to overcome their natural deficiencies (Getachew 2019; Manela 2007). In the League of Nations, self-government, independence and self-determination were articulated as both universal principles and as a stage of development. In order to access these principles, the colonies would first have to develop political structures and systems that the West recognised, rather than maintaining non-European systems that the West viewed as 'tribalistic' (Grovogui 1996).

Thereafter, the Covenant goes on to detail specific strategies for the maintenance of international peace and security. As stated in chapter 1, Article 8 of the Covenant asserts that 'the maintenance of peace requires the reduction of national armaments to the lowest point consistent with national safety' and that members of the League agree to 'interchange full and frank information as to the scale of their armaments, their military, naval and air programmes and the condition of such of their industries are adaptable to war-like purposes' (League of Nations 1919). This suggests that for states to interact peacefully with one another, there must be little possibility for military aggression. The Covenant, therefore, symbolised a commitment to a universal alliance of states, particularly with regard to issues around international peace and security, in place of the numerous and unsuccessful pre-First World War alliances – that Wilson had termed 'secret covenants' – between individual states.

In the same way as the United Nations after it, the League of Nations attempted to address the tension between state sovereignty and internationalism by requiring member states to forfeit some elements of their sovereignty in order to achieve international order through a commitment to international law and to systems and practices for handling disputes (Wilder 2015). As a result, member states were both sovereign and subject to international law. Where states were not yet considered sovereign, they were to be supervised through systems developed by the League of Nations as a collective rather than agreements between individual states or military forces. Given the centuries of colonial expansion that preceded the League of Nations and wars fought between imperial powers over colonial territories, this signified a shift in how international relations would manage those territories and how imperial states would engage with one another.

Where previous alliances had been between individual states or small groups of states, the League of Nations represented broader cooperation between nations with regard to the prevention of global conflict. In creating an international organisation of states in this way, the League of Nations had hoped that the most powerful nations would be able to work together to provide collective security on a larger scale than previously possible (MacQueen

2011). Nonetheless, as with any international institution, the reality and the ideal were poles apart. Although, in theory, the League of Nations was to be a universal coalition of states, the reality was that membership was limited and Eurocentric, giving no voice to those countries under colonial rule and providing a great deal of protection to the idea of national sovereignty (Schlesinger 2003). The League of Nations was, in practice, an agreement between the world's major powers of that time to prevent conflict on a similar scale to the First World War, while failing to address the inequalities inherent in the colonial system. Sovereignty, the maintenance of peace and respecting obligations not to resort to war were only applicable to those states that were already independent. Despite Wilson's bold and ambitious claims related to self-determination for the colonies, universality, in this case, did not apply to everyone.

Some elements of the League of Nations, in fact, actively encouraged the continuation of colonial rule, which is particularly apparent in an examination of the mandate system. As previously noted, the Covenant of the League of Nations established a system for dealing with territories that had previously been colonies of the defeated empires from the First World War. Article 22 states:

> To those colonies and territories which as a consequence of the late war have ceased to be under the sovereignty of the States which formerly governed them and which are inhabited by peoples not yet able to stand by themselves under the strenuous conditions of the modern world, there should be applied the principle that the well-being and development of such peoples form a sacred trust of civilisation and that securities for the performance of this trust should be embodied in this Covenant. (League of Nations 1919)

Rather than seeking independence for the colonies that had ceased to be under the control of their colonisers at the end of the war, the League of Nations developed a system that stated that 'the tutelage of such peoples should be entrusted to advanced nations who by reason of their resources, their experience or their geographical position can best undertake the responsibility, and who are willing to accept it' (League of Nations 1919). These former colonial territories were split into three categories: A, B and C mandates. A mandate consisted of the former colonies of the Ottoman Empire, such as Iraq, Palestine and Syria. Under Article 22 of the Covenant, these territories were considered to have 'reached a stage of development where their existence as independent nations can be provisionally recognized subject to the rendering of administrative advice and assistance by a Mandatory until such time as they are able to stand alone' (League of Nations 1919). These territories were considered 'developed' to the degree that they no longer required direct supervision from an imperial centre and could be recognised as independent states, although they would continue to receive 'assistance' from mandatory power. Category B mandates included Cameroon and Togo, German East Africa and Rwanda-Burundi and were subject to the full administrative control of the mandatory power (League of Nations 1919). Category B territories were considered to be at such an early stage in the development process that they required administrative supervision from imperial power and would be unable to make decisions regarding the running of their institutions. Finally, Category C mandates included territories such as South West Africa and the South Pacific Islands. These territories were to become 'integral portions' of the mandatory power's territory due to 'the sparseness of their population, or their small size, or their remoteness from the centres of civilization' (League of Nations 1919). These territories were either too small or too remote to be considered for independence by the League of Nations and were to be integrated into existing empires.

This system of control developed by the League of Nations to deal with colonial territories reinforces ideologies of civilisation and progress while attempting to disguise the relationship between these ideas and the violence of colonial rule. The mandate system signified the beginning of the move from an arrangement of direct colonial rule to a system of indirect colonial rule through the idea of development and collective administration (Rajagopal 2003). The distinction between category A, B and C mandates reiterates the understanding of civilisation as a linear progression, with those countries who are furthest away from European cultural values being subject to the strictest level of supervision and remote or sparse territories being fully integrated into empires due to the fear that they may never adhere to European values without such intense supervision. The very idea of 'tutelage' as outlined in Article 22 of the Covenant again reinforces this problematic notion of European culture as the height of civilisation and the idea that in order for these territories to be granted sovereignty, they must adopt European cultural values. The significance of the mandate system will become even more apparent in chapter 3, which provides an examination of the development of the United Nations as an institution and its desire to distance itself from the League of Nations and the question of colonialism. However, as Wilder (2015) notes, the mandate system is also significant in the way that it represents a new understanding of sovereignty. The mandate system created both non-sovereign states, that is, mandate territories that were not colonies as such but not sovereign either, and non-national sovereignty, that is, the status afforded to the League of Nations as the ultimate authority. Where sovereignty and the state are usually understood as two intricately intertwined concepts, the mandate system sees sovereignty exist separately from the idea of the state. Thus, sovereignty as a concept was able to adapt itself to a new global order that would enable the continuation of colonial power dynamics, albeit in a revised format. Former colonial territories now sat somewhere in between a colony and a sovereign state, while the League of Nations was able to present itself as the ultimate sovereign.

This contradiction is also apparent in the League of Nations' treatment of states that were not colonies but not considered sovereign. As noted in the previous chapter, the case of Ethiopia is instructive in demonstrating the elasticity of the concept of sovereignty. At the time of the League's founding, Ethiopia was recognised as a state and could not be managed under the mandate system. Instead, the League granted conditional membership with an agreement that Ethiopia would be subject to supervision by European powers to ensure particular standards of 'civilization' (Donaldson 2020). As such, Ethiopia came to occupy a position as both sovereign and not-sovereign simultaneously (Parfitt 2011). Sovereignty in this context was not understood as a status that one either had or did not have, but one that could be granted conditionally, and thus, a hierarchy of sovereignties was entrenched in the League of Nations. The consequences of this for Ethiopia were severe in that it suffered Italian annexation in the mid-1930s. As Parfitt (2011) notes, the rights and protections available to Ethiopia within the League were weaker than those of its European counterparts, showing that sovereignty in this context was never intended to be a universal principle applying to all states equally. European member states would always remain the ultimate sovereigns, and the League's treatment of both mandate territories and independent non-European states reveals the extent to which this project sought to entrench international hierarchy.

THE LEAGUE AGAINST IMPERIALISM

While the League of Nations is usually remembered in relation to the Treaty of Versailles, and as the first attempt at an international organisation of states, another story is less often told. At the same time that the Paris Peace Conference was taking place and in the years between the First and Second World Wars, Paris also became a significant meeting point for anti-colonial activists. International anti-colonial groups saw Paris as a meaningful location that allowed space to discuss both issues of international politics and issues related to their territories (Goebel 2015). Anti-colonial activists saw a need to establish a presence within Europe in order to respond to the international politics that so often took place on European soil, so although their primary focus was on decolonisation outside of Europe, Paris became a hub for anti-colonial resistance in order to maintain a direct connection to those European states that were responsible for colonial oppression. This would also help engage and garner support from European anti-colonial activists, some of whom were notable public figures (Albert Einstein perhaps most famously).

The failure of Wilson to follow through on his commitments to self-determination and sovereignty for the colonies and the subsequent implementation of the mandate system made it clear that the League of Nations would not dramatically change the situation of those living under colonial rule. As such, the Paris Peace Conference only served to fuel existing anti-colonial sentiment and the desire for full decolonisation and independence. This is despite the attempts of anti-colonial activists to make demands upon European colonising powers at the Paris Conference. For example, Marcus Garvey was in attendance on behalf of the Universal Negro Improvement Association (UNIA) and argued that, among other moves towards equality, the principle of self-determination that was central to Wilson's proposals ought also to apply to Africa and all colonies controlled by European powers (Persaud 2016). As Persaud (2016) noted, the conference provided a focal point for anti-colonial activists grounded in a sense of transnational solidarity, a shared history of oppression and a belief in the sovereignty of people and their lands. The League against Imperialism was one of the earliest attempts to unify this anti-colonial anger into a formal organisation. Its chosen name signified a direct attack on the League of Nations and the preservation of imperialism that was represented by the mandate system (Prashad 2007). Evidently, the mandate system did not represent the decolonisation or independence that the colonies had been hopeful for prior to the Paris Peace Conference, and so the League against Imperialism was a direct reaction to the continued colonial domination being legitimised by the League of Nations.

The need to be free of colonial domination in any and every way possible, therefore, became a key feature of anti-colonial resistance at the end of the First World War (Chakrabarty, 2010). The unfulfilled promise of Wilson's plan had proved that it was not possible to negotiate with imperial powers and their militarily powerful allies. However, the relationship between Wilson's Fourteen Points, the Paris Peace Conference and the anti-colonial movement has often been neglected within historical accounts of the development of international institutions, even where they are critical of the League. In narrating the agreements made at the Paris Peace Conference and the development of the League of Nations, the anti-colonial movement has been relatively understudied until recent years. As Manela (2006) argues, historians of international relations have been inclined to ignore the very issues ignored by the allied powers at the conference, namely the demands for decolonisation from peoples outside of Europe that were contrary to the interests of the major powers. To neglect this tension in historical accounts of the Paris Peace Conference or accounts of the signing of the Treaty of Versailles suggests an unwillingness to deal with the role of colonialism in the building of the

League of Nations as an institution and neglects a long history of resistance that was very much present. The remainder of this chapter will address this gap by discussing archival material from the League against Imperialism and engagement with more recent literature that has sought to address this gap.

The League against Imperialism was established at the first International Congress against Colonial Oppression and Imperialism, which opened on 10 February 1927, and saw 174 delegates representing organisations from thirty-four countries gather together in Brussels. The provisional organising committee included representatives from China, India, Egypt, Mexico, Germany, France, England, the USA and South America, who sent out invitations to attend alongside a provisional agenda, which contained four primary points for discussion, as follows:

1. Reports on imperialist oppression in the colonies and in countries, menaced in their independence;
2. The emancipation movement of the oppressed nations and the support to be given by the labour movement and the progressive parties in the imperialist countries;
3. The co-ordination of the forces of the national emancipation movement with the forces of the labour movement as well as the imperialist countries;
4. The building of a permanent international organization in order to link up all forces combating international imperialism and in order to ensure their effective support for the fight of emancipation conducted by oppressed nations. (LAIA, ARCH00804.1, IIH)

The first congress was centred around identifying streams of support and solidarity across the world and within imperial states, as well as beginning the task of building an international organisation that would rival the League of Nations. Those present at the congress were not limited to national leaders from the colonies or former colonies but significant figures from around the globe who had made clear their support for the anti-colonial project, from academics to trade union leaders. The Brussels Congress provided a challenge to existing conceptions of the world by rejecting the 'civilizing mission' that had been used as a justification for colonisation throughout history (Louro 2018).

Attendees at the first congress included – but were by no means limited to – representatives from the NAACP (USA); workers' movements from Mexico, USA, Cuba, Venezuela, China, India and France; student federations from Cuba, Mexico, Peru, China, Korea and India; Trade Unions from England, Mexico, India and South Africa; and the Women's International League for Peace from Germany, England and France. From the outset, the League against Imperialism sought to unite the strengths of a wide range of organisations working against oppression in its various forms. These connections between anti-imperialism, workers' rights, women's rights and the student movement are significant in that they demonstrate that the sentiment of the League against Imperialism was not simply anti-imperialist but anti-capitalist too. Attendance at the Brussels Congress reflects that very few constraints were applied in determining membership of the League against Imperialism (Louro 2018). In contrast to the League of Nations, the League against Imperialism was accommodating of any and all individuals and groups who were defined as anti-imperialist. Its anti-capitalist focus was also in no small part a consequence of the Comintern's involvement in the organisation. As Petersson (2014) has detailed, the League against Imperialism provided a 'hub' for the Comintern to establish direct relationships with the colonies to garner worldwide support for communism.

These solidarities seen at the League against Imperialism's first congress were based on the understanding that colonialism is not simply about power and control but about exploitation for profit. As Walter Rodney states, 'colonialism was not merely a system of exploitation, but one whose essential purpose was to repatriate the profits to the so-called mother country' (2012 [1972], 149). The processes of appropriation, extraction and dispossession that accompanied colonisation were implemented to generate profit for imperial states and ensure that the colonies were tied into a global capitalist system that primarily benefitted the empire and imperial centres. Rodney's (1972) seminal text clearly and unequivocally demonstrates that European colonisation, particularly in Africa, was not intended to develop the African continent as some history books would have us believe, but rather that it intended to systematically *underdevelop* Africa through extraction that generated the most profit possible, as is the aim of capitalism. Infrastructure was developed only where it enabled the movement of raw materials for manufacturing in Europe. Put simply: 'All roads and railways led down to the sea' (Rodney 1972, 209). Therefore, it makes sense that a movement that is anti-colonial or anti-imperial would also be anti-capitalist. However, the League against Imperialism also employed a more expansive understanding of the relationship between imperialism and capitalism, arguing that political control via formal colonisation was not necessary for imperialism. The Brussels Congress highlighted the struggles against imperialism in technically independent countries – namely China, India, and Mexico – to show that imperial exploitation did not only happen via formal colonisation but also through dependence on capitalism (Louro 2018). The Congress Manifesto of the League against Imperialism's first congress projects this strongly anti-capitalist message through references to 'involuntary victims of foreign capitalist exploitation' and calls to follow 'the historical example of the Workers' State which rests upon the ruins of this house of oppression, lights up like a torch the path of the struggle for freedom of the oppressed and enslaved nations' (LAIA, ARCH00804.10, IISH). The League against Imperialism saw capitalism and imperialism as inherently intertwined and the destruction of both as necessary and connected.

Indicated by the list of attendees alone, the congress, therefore, fostered a strong sense of solidarity among all those subject to oppression under capitalism, and in establishing the organisation, the manifesto states:

> Under these conditions, this Brussels Conference has decided to found the 'League Against Imperialism and for National Independence'. We announce to all oppressed people and all oppressed classes of the dominating nations, the foundation of this League. We appeal to all who do not profit from the oppression of others and who do not live on the fruits of this oppression, and to all who hate modern slavery and are longing for their own freedom and the freedom of their fellow-men, to affiliate to us and to support us. (LAIA, ARCH00804.10, IISH)

This appeal in the manifesto calls out not only the oppressed in the colonies but the oppressed in 'dominating nations' to support the League against Imperialism and its opposition to the League of Nations. These documents sought to connect activists on a global scale from various political positions (Brückenhaus 2017). Anti-colonialism was not restricted to those living in existing or former colonies, and the League against Imperialism sought to gather support from those within imperial states who nonetheless supported the cause or suffered under this international order.

The second congress, which met two years later, from 20 July to 31 July 1929, had a similar focus on the need to unite anti-colonial forces with workers' movements and trade unions. In a piece entitled *The Trade Unions and the Struggle against Imperialism*, it is argued that 'the class trade unions represent the best basis for real anti-imperialist struggle and thus for the development of the League Against Imperialism' (LAIA, ARCH00804.89, IISH). The League against Imperialism saw their best hope of developing a strong resistance movement as grounded in the solidarity of already existing international networks of the working classes. This meant uniting the working classes of the colonies and the working classes globally. The piece states that:

> In so far as the main task of the League Against Imperialism is to achieve absolute independence for the colonies, it should and can cooperate only with those trade union organisations in the capitalist and colonial countries, which do not merely pay lip service, but which really fight against all forms of colonial oppression and slavery and stand for the complete independence of the colonial and semi-colonial countries. He who is opposed to independence for the colonial countries is a servant of imperialism. (LAIA, ARCH00804.89, IISH)

The League against Imperialism's position was clear: anti-capitalism and anti-colonialism go hand in hand, but workers' movements involved in the League against Imperialism must support full independence for all of the colonies. They could not allow the anti-colonial movement to be co-opted for the purposes of the anti-capitalist struggle and solidarity between the two had to meet the needs of both.

While these two struggles had much in common in terms of the cause of their inequalities, this same statement is also clear, however, in distinguishing between the working classes of the colonies and the working classes of Europe, arguing that 'the working class of the colonial and semi-colonial countries has to fight against a double oppression. Against the pressure of the imperialists and that of the native bourgeoisie' (LAIA, ARCH00804.89, IISH). As many scholars have noted, both prior to and since this congress, the working classes of the colonies faced a battle for independence not only against their colonisers but also against those from within the colonies who were keen to maintain colonial power structures after decolonisation. In Fanon's analysis, the colonialist bourgeoisie – that is, the bourgeoisie of colonising countries – use the elite within the colonies to continue imperial control through a 'rearguard campaign in the fields of culture, values and technology' (1967, 9). As such, the working classes of the colonies have to fight both against the coloniser and against those who have succumbed to the understanding of the coloniser's culture as 'universal' or 'civilised' culture. So, while the working classes of Europe provided a useful avenue for support, their struggles were markedly different in that the absence of a colonial power meant that they only faced single oppression based on class rather than class and race. Statements made at the 1929 Congress in line with this view signified a further ideological shift to the left, reflecting the increased communist membership and Comintern involvement (Brückenhaus 2017).

The archives of the League against Imperialism also serve as an important reminder that imperialism was not solely a relationship between Europe and Africa or Asia. They detail the ongoing colonisation and neocolonisation of Latin America by the United States and stress the significant role Latin American states played in anti-colonial movements. A speech made by José Vasconcelos – the former education secretary for Mexico – emphasised the extent to which Latin America was still suffering at the hands of imperialism despite formal independence:

> We started in Latin America as colonies of Spanish and Portuguese and we are very far from being free at present. It seems that our fate is to remain as colonies. [. . .] Few people take the pains to look at the map and see how that tremendous Empire, U.S.A. has been built up – through robbery, through bravery, through

cruelty and through cleverness, but this miracle endangers the whole of humanity. (LAIA, ARCH00804.39, IISH)

Vasconcelos' speech discusses the economic difficulties facing Latin America post-independence, particularly in relation to the ownership of land. During this period, significant portions of Latin American land and resources were bought by North American trusts developing the technology to farm for profit. The land had been bought cheaply as it was relatively fruitless without the technology required to farm it, but this would be a profitable long-term investment once the technology had been established. These economic concerns raised by Latin American delegates at the conference reinforced the tangled struggles of anti-imperialism and anti-capitalism and the extent to which independence was an insufficient solution to addressing the reach of imperial power. In addressing those still under colonial rule, Vasconcelos says simply: 'Our struggle is like yours – a battle for progress and justice' (LAIA, ARCH00804.39, IISH).

The League against Imperialism brought together a range of groups from different circumstances but with a common enemy. They sought to counter the weight of the League of Nations with an organisation that was substantially more global in its focus, and that pushed for decolonisation that would address the relationship between imperialism and capitalism. This consolidation of transnational solidarity through a central organisation represented a significant moment in the history of international institutions. As Petersson (2014) notes, the League against Imperialism was more successful than any other interwar organisation in bringing together a wide variety of organisations and individuals to fight against imperialism. The activities of the League against Imperialism sought to challenge colonialism and European hegemony via the 'civilizing mission', instead of arguing that a working-class alliance of colonised peoples and the Soviet Union would enhance global development for all (Louro 2018). The history of the League of Nations is most often written from the perspective of European politics, without acknowledging the extent to which this was a project of collaboration between empires. To recognise a concurrent and intricately connected history of anti-colonial resistance alters our understanding of the power dynamics contained within it.

UNIVERSALISM AND INTERNATIONALISM

Despite the claims being made around internationalism and universalism at the end of the First World War, President Wilson's inaction at the Peace Conference had resulted in a pessimistic response to the discourse of universalism among colonial peoples and anti-colonial activists (Goebel 2015). Wilson's statements on self-determination and giving equal weight to the interests of populations concerned did little to improve the situation of those living under colonialism. Rather, it quickly became clear that the universalism and respect for sovereignty that the major powers discussed in their plans for the League of Nations were not designed to include the colonies. While the major powers discussed a need for international relations based on a 'universal brotherhood' and Western understandings of universalism, it was apparent that this brotherhood would not extend beyond European borders (Goebel 2015). Understanding that the League of Nations embedded colonial power structures and ensured their perpetuation through systems that relied upon discourses of development and Eurocentric ideas of civilisation is an important basis for understanding the functioning of the United Nations in later years and the ability for international institutions to make claims to universality while maintaining the power dynamics of colonialism.

The discussion in this chapter has demonstrated the flexibility of the concept of sovereignty that has been essential to both the League of Nations and the United Nations and, in doing so, demonstrates the ways in which selectivity has been central to international politics. Discussions of the mandate system here have also provided a critical analysis of the concept of responsibility and how this has been utilised as a means of sustaining colonial power dynamics. Taken together, these two issues begin to explain the conceptual relevance of *selective responsibility*, whereby the major powers have established international systems that allow them to maintain control (via the concept of responsibility) but apply principles and policies selectively. It is also important, however, to recognise that this has been both acknowledged and resisted historically in order to expand our capacity for the critical assessment of contemporary issues. The League against Imperialism provides an example of the possibilities of transnational solidarities and recognises the power of the West in terms of resisting resistance and keeping this history out of dominant narratives. The understandably cynical response to the inherent contradictions of imperialist states championing universalism from proponents of anti-colonialism was particularly present in the League against Imperialism, and this provides an important starting point for the tradition of anti-colonial resistance to the United Nations that is central to this book. An examination of the archives of the League against Imperialism provides an alternative vision for internationalism that would be both anti-colonial and anti-capitalist. This chapter provides important historical context for the debates outlined in chapter 3 to resist the narrative of rupture associated with the establishment of the United Nations. It has explored the complexities of anti-colonial organising in the interwar period and essential critiques of the concepts of sovereignty and self-determination that filter through to discussions of a 'new' organisation after the Second World War and the need for caution in addressing claims of universalism in the international context.

Chapter 3

The United Nations and Colonialism

Re-narrating San Francisco

The Second World War was the final straw for the League of Nations and the ultimate signal that it had failed to prevent conflict on a global scale. As outlined in chapter 1, the standard narrative follows that the League of Nations disbanded and the United Nations was established in response to the end of the Second World War. This narrative allows for a framing of the United Nations as an organisation committed to equality and universal rights, aiming for a more inclusive global membership. It enables an inaccurate framing of the United Nations as the beginning of the end of colonialism and empire. This chapter argues that to see a rupture between the two organisations disguises the significance of colonialism in the founding of the United Nations. Using archival data from the United Nations' own archive that is less often addressed in the literature, this chapter explores the refusal of the major powers to address the issue of colonialism during the San Francisco conference of 1945 that ended with the signing of the Charter of the United Nations. Related to this, this chapter delves into the decisions around the structure of the United Nations Security Council that were highly contested, as shown by the archives.

In doing so, it presents an alternative historical narrative that reveals the extent of the power and privilege of the major powers in establishing the United Nations and in constructing an organisation that would prevent the possibility of decisions that were not in their interests. As suggested in the introduction, the structures of the United Nations that institutionalised the privilege of the world's major powers utilised a language of responsibility as justification. This chapter shows that the structures established in San Francisco enable the major powers to exercise this responsibility selectively, which in turn calls into question the extent to which the United Nations can be understood as a break from the colonial past. It also seeks to challenge the historical silencing of anti-colonial resistance that plays a key role in the continued domination of the global south, questioning the motives of the major powers and beginning to question the role of key discursive concepts such as development, progress and responsibility that continue to frame international relations today, while also reinforcing the importance of reading these contemporary dynamics through this colonial history.

THE COLONIAL QUESTION AT SAN FRANCISCO

In the later years of the League of Nations and prior to the United Nations Conference on International Organisation (UNCIO) at San Francisco, there was a shift in public attitudes away from support for colonialism. The European colonial powers faced the rising strength of independence movements within colonial territories, and this shift in public attitudes both within and outside of Europe made the maintenance of colonial rule difficult to uphold (Matz 2005). Despite this, the founding members of the United Nations managed to keep questions around colonialism and decolonisation to a minimum during the conference in 1945. As chapter 1 showed, this silencing of the issue of colonialism is something that has been replicated throughout standard accounts of the history of the United Nations, and the standard historical narrative suggests that the issue of colonialism was dealt with at the San Francisco conference, with the universalism of United Nations membership signifying an end to empire and colonialism as we knew it. Not only does this narrative fail to acknowledge how certain countries came to be the major powers and the key players in the United Nations in the first instance, but it is also highly deceptive in terms of concealing the ways in which colonial questions were (not) dealt with at San Francisco. Marika Sherwood puts this plainly when she states that

> not one of the innumerable books on the founding of the United Nations at San Francisco fifty years ago mentions the efforts made by colonized peoples and black Americans to have their voices heard and to have the freeing of the colonies put on the UN's agenda. (1996, 71)

These standard histories, such as those detailed in chapter 1, highlight the problem of selective membership as one of the main failures of the League of Nations and even recognise the fact that the four sponsoring countries present at the Dumbarton Oaks Conference (the United Kingdom, the United States, China and the Soviet Union) claimed that they were 'not ready' to discuss the issue of colonialism and moves towards decolonisation (Gilchrist 1945). However, they do not address the anti-colonial resistance that was present both prior to and at the moment of the establishment of the United Nations. This narrative suggests that the discussion of colonialism was down to the sponsoring countries, which were unwilling to engage in any sort of meaningful debate, and as such this narrative fails to acknowledge the work of those anti-colonial activists that was being outright ignored by the sponsoring governments in their decision to not discuss decolonisation.

Although the sponsors wished to frame the United Nations as a new organisation that would succeed where the League of Nations had failed, the issue of colonialism and colonial independence at Dumbarton Oaks did not appear to feature as a high priority or proved to be such a contentious issue that the colonial powers wished to avoid it altogether in order to protect their own political interests. The question of colonial territories was sidelined, to be dealt with at San Francisco, and the agreements made here were to be embodied in the Charter (Nicholas 1975). However, in reality, discussions on working papers at San Francisco did not allow for any radical amendments at all by smaller states, not least radical amendments on colonialism (Hurd 2007). The discussion of how to manage the colonial territories was limited to a discussion between colonial powers rather than a discussion involving the subjects of the empire or representatives of ex-colonial territories. In the standard historical narratives, the absence of colonialism in the discussions at Dumbarton Oaks and at San Francisco is frequently put down to disagreements between the major powers or the fact that the focus was on creating an international institution rather than dealing with colonialism.

Therefore, the significant absence of discussions of colonialism at San Francisco is rarely put into the context of the anti-colonial movement that existed concurrently. As Plummer (2003) argues, the United Nations acted as an early forum for debates around human rights and civil rights, particularly for African American activists, who raised concerns around the content of the Charter as well as the representation of minorities and women at the conference. The colonial question was absent from the agenda at San Francisco, but this is not to say that attempts were not made to raise the issues of colonialism and decolonisation. A number of anti-colonial groups expressed a desire to address the issues of decolonisation and sovereign equality for all territories involved in the organisation – as they had in the years following the establishment of the League of Nations – but the Western powers showed no desire to discuss these issues, instead wishing to protect their own sovereignty and the rights of their own states above all else (Patil 2008). Within this context, this meant their right to rule over colonial territories and govern over these territories without the interference of international bodies. Despite the reluctance of the major powers to address the issue of colonialism, prior to the conference in San Francisco, attempts were made by individuals and groups external to the planning of the conference to

ensure equal representation at San Francisco and get decolonisation put on
the agenda. These attempts, however, have been written out of the standard
histories of the United Nations, and these standard histories, therefore,
signify a failure to deal with the colonial history of the United Nations as
an institution and a neglect of significant debates around its founding. There
has, however, been important work done to counteract this silencing (see,
for example, Plummer 1996, 2003; Anderson 1996, 2003, 2015; Sherwood
1996), but these accounts do not form the dominant narrative, or this activism
is seen as somehow separate to the conference. The aim here is to contribute
to this de-silencing of anti-colonial narratives through the examination of
archival material from the conference itself.

ANTI-COLONIALISM IN SAN FRANCISCO

The African Academy of Arts and Research is one such example of a group
that attempted to get decolonisation put onto the agenda at the San Francisco
conference. It was established in 1943 by three African students studying
in America – Kingsley Mbadiwe, Mbonu Ojike and A. A. Nwafor Orizu –
with the aim of promoting African independence. During the San Francisco
conference in 1945, Ojike lobbied extensively for target dates to be set on
African independence but was unable to secure a meeting with either British
or American representatives (Diamond 2005). A joint letter from the African
Academy of Arts and Research and the African Students Association, which
enclosed a 'Memorandum of Recommendations on Independence of British
West African Colonies', was met with the response from United Nations
information officer T. T. McCrosky that

> the Conference is devoting its energies and its labors exclusively to the single
> problem of setting up an international organization to maintain peace and
> security and therefore it is not anticipated that the specific problems mentioned
> in the memorandums will be the subject of action. (Letter from T.T. McCrosky
> to Mr Ojike, 30 May 1945)

This response suggests that colonialism was in no way related to the issue
of international peace and security and highlights the overwhelming desire
of the European empires to keep the issue of colonialism out of discussions
in San Francisco despite mounting public pressure. However, it is interesting
in itself that, as Sherwood (1996) points out, attempts such as this to put
decolonisation on the agenda at San Francisco are rarely included in the
standard histories of the United Nations, and in telling its own history the
United Nations does not acknowledge this as an issue.

Similarly, the president of the West Indies National Council Dr Charles A. Petioni and Vice President Richard B. Moore lobbied the San Francisco conference on behalf of Caribbean interests, arguing that British colonial rule in the West Indies was not acting in the interests of encouraging self-government and that the resources of the West Indies were being used to produce profit for the European powers controlling them (Turner and Turner 1988). The response to Moore's 'Appeal on Behalf of the Caribbean Peoples', which was circulated to government officials in San Francisco states that:

> You are of course aware that the purpose of the San Francisco Conference is to formulate the best possible charter for an international organization to maintain peace and security for all people of the world regardless of race, color, religion or sex. It will devote its energies and its labors exclusively to this task, and it is not intended that the matter you mention will be the subject of action here. (Letter from Alger Hiss to Mr Moore, 1 June 1945)

Again, this response is remarkably contradictory. In raising questions about the exploitation of people and resources in colonial territories, representatives of the West Indies National Council are told that these questions are not appropriate questions to be raised in the context of developing an international organisation for the maintenance of peace and security. This standard response is seen repeatedly in reply to letters from organisations such as the National Committee for India's Freedom (Letter from Alger Hiss to Mrs Pandit, May 11, 1945), the Lithuanian League of Canada (Letter from T. T. McCrosky to Mr Batkus, May 6, 1945) and the movement for Indonesian independence (Letter from T. T. McCrosky to Mr Patty, May 23, 1945), among others. In the same vein, letters from individuals arguing for the importance of black representation in San Francisco are met with the response that:

> No special group interest as such has a delegation to the Conference. Their interests are represented by their respective national delegations. The Delegation of the United States, for example, has a number of unofficial consultants from special groups that were invited to send representatives to San Francisco, among them the Association for the Advancement of Colored People. There is also a prominent Negro on the staff of that Delegation. You are also aware no doubt that the Delegates of certain other countries are of the Negro race. (Letter from T. T. McCrosky to Mrs Black, 21 May 1945)

As referenced in the text above, the National Association for the Advancement of Colored People (NAACP) did send Walter White, Mary McLeod Bethune and W. E. B. Du Bois as representatives in the American delegation at San Francisco to raise issues of representation and independence for the colonies, as well as racial equality more generally. Out of the forty-two organisations invited to act as consultants to the US delegation at the conference, the NAACP was the only group selected to represent the interests of the African American population (Anderson 2003). Ultimately, the goals they had set themselves in attending the conference were unfulfilled by the time the conference came to a close, and, in fact, despite including them in the conference to represent the interests of so-called special interest groups, the colonial powers and the American delegation made it clear to the representatives of the NAACP that the language of sovereignty and self-determination was not applicable to people of the colonial territories (Tillery 2011).

This is not to say that the NAACP did not organise and attempt to make their voices heard. Prior to the conference, Du Bois made contact with a number of black activists including Nwafor Orizu of the African Academy of Arts and Research, to organise a separate conference before the actual San Francisco conference to prepare the NAACP representatives (Anderson 1996). This pre-conference conference concluded with the following four key points that were taken forward by the NAACP representatives to San Francisco:

1. Colonialism must go;
2. The transition from colonial status to autonomy should be overseen by an international body;
3. Colonials should be represented on this international body;
4. The primary objective should be to improve the social and economic conditions of colonial peoples. (Sherwood 1996, 77)

In spite of Du Bois's efforts and his preparation for the San Francisco conference, his interventions were ultimately unproductive. The Charter that came out of the conference and that still guides the actions of the United Nations today failed to address decolonisation in any concrete manner, and the inclusion of the NAACP in the US consultant organisations appeared to be decorative rather than actually allowing for any form of debate or impact (Anderson 2003). In fact, the US delegation resisted the inclusion of any significant references to racial inequality or discrimination in the Charter (Lauren 2003).

Despite the issues of empire and decolonisation being raised by these various organisations both prior to and during the conference in San Francisco, their attempts and the unsatisfactory responses from the conference organisers are seldom mentioned in the standard history of the United Nations. To exclude these significant exchanges and debates from the historical understanding of the development of the United Nations as an institution is clearly problematic, and as Getachew argues, 'By framing the UN as the embodiment of a "new deal for the world" that needed only to be expanded, anticolonial nationalism and decolonisation are assimilated into a progressive history of postwar ideals and institutions' (2019, 75). The history told by the United Nations itself and reproduced by academics in the seventy years since its establishment fails to acknowledge the ways in which the basic structure of the organisation, and even the structure and content of the conference understood to be its birthplace, ignores particular aspects of history and particular power relationships. Processes such as this allow for the legitimation of the institutionalisation of great power privilege, which is exceptional in the case of the United Nations as compared with other international institutions (Krisch 2008). To accept these standard histories as accurate representations of the development of the United Nations fails to understand that history is a construction, not just a factual record of events.

PERMANENT MEMBERSHIP AND POSTCOLONIAL PRIVILEGE

Nowhere is this hierarchical ordering more present than in the Security Council. The power afforded to the permanent members of the Security Council had been a contentious issue at San Francisco for a number of member states and those anti-colonial groups who were struggling to be heard. Prior to the San Francisco conference, the structure of the Security Council had been discussed and debated at length by the sponsoring nations, and in reality the discussions at San Francisco were unlikely to have a significant impact. As such, it is important to recognise what the initial disagreements were and how the decisions around the structure of the Security Council were justified despite intense resistance to the creation of an organisation that would reproduce the power dynamics of colonialism.

As outlined in chapter 1, the Dumbarton Oaks Conference, more formally known as the Washington Conversations on International Peace and Security Organization, took place between 21 August and 7 October 1944. The conference consisted of representatives from the United Kingdom, the United States, the Soviet Union and China. Following on from the earlier international conferences towards the end of the Second World War, the aim of the Dumbarton Oaks Conference was to formally propose an international organisation that would prevent the outbreak of another World War, learning from the lessons of the League of Nations which had failed to do so. The League of Nations had been deemed a failure publicly and internationally as a result of the Second World War, and so these key players in the international community had begun work on a new organisation as a replacement. This section will outline some of the power politics at play in the initial stages of the United Nations' development, particularly in relation to the

Security Council and its five permanent members, drawing on the work of historian Robert C. Hilderbrand who has written extensively about this in his 1990 book *Dumbarton Oaks: The Origins of the United Nations and the Search for Postwar Security*. These discussions at Dumbarton Oaks were particularly important in terms of framing the debate that would occur at San Francisco, whereby both anti-colonial organisations and potential member states opposed the power that would be afforded to the sponsoring nations.

The overwhelming failure of the League of Nations had been attributed in no small part to the absence of two of the world's greatest powers at that time: the United States and the Soviet Union. As Hilderbrand (1990) argues, their involvement was deemed essential to address the failures of the League and for a new organisation to succeed. Where the League of Nations had been selective in its membership, this new organisation was imagined to be much more inclusive and aimed to unite a larger number of the world's governments, but more specifically to unite the most powerful. From the perspective of the United States itself, however, this involvement in a new international organisation was also part of a broader political campaign. President Roosevelt saw this as an opportunity to justify the US involvement in the Second World War, framing it as a longer-term project to contribute to the maintenance of international peace and security (Hilderbrand 1990). For the United States, a new international organisation would justify to the public their contribution to the war by framing it as the beginning of a united international attempt to bring about world peace. Already it is clear that the involvement of particular states in the creation of the United Nations did not simply stem from a desire to create a better world. Rather, the involvement of the major powers of the United Nations was also politically motivated. Each of the governments invited to take part in the meetings at Dumbarton Oaks brought with them proposals for an international organisation, and these were debated over the course of the conference. These discussions eventually resulted in the 'Dumbarton Oaks Documents on International Organization' that were taken to the San Francisco conference and formed the basis of the Charter of the United Nations. This conference and the resulting documents show the ways in which the privilege of the world's most powerful nations was built into the United Nations from the outset, particularly in relation to the Security Council and the ways in which the organisation was imagined to deal with future international conflicts.

While preliminary discussions on the development of an international organisation prior to Dumbarton Oaks had largely been between Britain, the United States and the Soviet Union, the United Nations Security Council eventually came to be dominated – and still is dominated – by five permanent members, with the additions of France and China. This permanent membership within the Security Council confirms the status of these nations as great powers, but in the case of France, in particular, the symbolism of permanent membership may have *granted* great power status (Krisch 2008). The perceived status and privilege of these nations were now to be institutionalised in the form of the Security Council. Their role as permanent members simultaneously cemented their power and legitimated it by framing these five states as the key players in maintaining international peace and security. Although not present at the Dumbarton Oaks Conference, France was given a key role in the new organisation at the insistence of the British government. According to Hilderbrand (1990), regardless of their perceived shortcomings during the Second World War, Winston Churchill insisted that France be given a permanent seat on the Security Council amid fears that Britain would otherwise face the power of the Soviet Union alone or else rely on the support of the United States, which was not always guaranteed. Churchill believed that France would provide Britain with the support required to stand up to two of the world's most powerful states to emerge after the First World War.

The permanent membership of China was also a strategic decision, however, in this instance, on the part of the United States. As Hilderbrand's (1990) account states, while China was not at the time considered to be a global power on the same scale as the United States, the Soviet Union or the United Kingdom, their involvement was deemed to be essential by the United States, whose own involvement was essential for the organisation to work at all. In the British government's view, the inclusion of China in the plans for an international organisation was a political initiative on the part of President Roosevelt, with plans to guide China to a position where it would be strong enough to police Asia but weak enough to still rely on the United States. The United States wished to give China the international status that would enable them to control the rest of the Asian continent, while also creating a strong relationship between China and the United States. Even the inclusion of particular states as permanent members of the Security Council, and therefore as key players in the international organisation more generally, were strategic decisions based on the political interests of the United Kingdom and the United States with aims to support decisions that the other permanent members may challenge.

Unlike France, representatives from China were present at Dumbarton Oaks, although not at the same time as the Soviet Union. Although Chinese representatives took part in discussions at Dumbarton Oaks, the talks between British, American and Chinese representatives that took place in the latter days of the conference were ceremonial to a large degree, as the majority of the significant decisions had been made during talks with the Soviet Union. Even initial decisions about which countries should form the leadership of this new international organisation were, therefore, built around political relationships, ensuring that the interests of the Russians, the Americans and the British would be prioritised at all times. These five nations would become permanent members of the Security Council, dominating decisions around international intervention and holding primary responsibility for the maintenance of international peace and security. Therefore, it is no surprise that the attitude of the sponsoring governments was very much that the United Nations as an organisation was theirs and that it would preserve a world order that they would be the main beneficiaries of (Goodwin 1971).

The final documents of the Dumbarton Oaks Conference formed the basis for the agenda at the San Francisco conference between April and June 1945, where the Charter of the United Nations was signed, and it is worth emphasising here some of the key elements of the opening statements. The proposals were drafted and made public by the US representatives in the interests of enabling full discussion by the people of the United States prior to the San Francisco conference (United States 1944). These proposals state that the purpose of the new international organisation – from here on referred to as the United Nations – was 'to maintain international peace and security; and to that end to take collective measures for the prevention and removal of threats to the peace and the suppression of acts of aggression' (United States 1944, 8). They go on to state that to achieve this primary purpose, the United Nations would be 'based on the principle of the sovereign equality of all peace-loving states' (United States 1944, 8).

As previously noted, the United Nations was to be framed as an international body for collective action based on the fundamental equality of all its members. However, this principle of equality already appears to be in conflict both with the structure of the organisation and the very fact that the proposals upon which it was based were determined by a small number of states whose power and status were privileged above all others. Even when we consider the larger conference at San Francisco, forty-five nations in total were invited to attend, including nineteen from the Americas and the Caribbean, seven from Asia and the Middle East, ten from Europe and only three from Africa, which was largely still colonised (Bosco 2009). Despite claims to inclusivity and equality, this new organisation failed to address the issue of colonialism, and indeed, those participating at Dumbarton Oaks had claimed to be 'not ready' to discuss colonialism at this point (Gilchrist 1945, 983). As we saw in chapter 2 with the League of Nations, claims of inclusivity and internationalism, therefore, seemed only to apply to countries that fit traditional understandings of sovereignty, and colonised nations were not considered significant in proposals for a global organisation. If the United Nations were to be dominated by those present at the Dumbarton Oaks Conference, how could it be based on any notion of equality? This contradiction becomes even more apparent when we look at the decisions made around the structure of the Security Council and the powers that would be afforded to its members.

The Dumbarton Oaks proposals state that with regards to its composition:

> The Security Council should consist of one representative of each of eleven members of the organization. Representatives of the United States of America, the United Kingdom of Great Britain and Northern Ireland, the Union of Soviet Socialist Republics, the Republic of China, and, in due course, France, should have permanent seats. The General Assembly should elect six states to fill the non-permanent seats. These six states should be elected for a term of two years, three retiring each year. (United States 1944, 12)

The Security Council was to be made up of a combination of permanent and non-permanent members, with non-permanent members rotating to give more member states the opportunity to participate in Security Council decision-making. This proposed structure was agreed upon in the Charter and remained in place until reforms in 1965, which saw the non-permanent members of the Security Council increase from six to ten, although no reforms were made in terms of permanent membership. Although the inclusion of four additional non-permanent members could be seen as an attempt to increase representativeness and balance, this reform did little to address the major concerns around permanent membership. The United Nations, like the League of Nations before it, relied on a conceptualisation of sovereignty that enabled hierarchical ordering (Getachew 2019). The Security Council, which has always been viewed as the key body of the United Nations in terms of addressing threats to peace and security, was, therefore, dominated by powerful nations from the outset, and no reforms since 1945 have effectively addressed this issue. This in itself suggests an unwillingness to adopt the United Nations to more adequately reflect the contemporary world, instead maintaining a structure that legitimises the power of those who dominated global politics at the end of the Second World War.

At Dumbarton Oaks, the privilege to be afforded to the permanent members of the Security Council was central, with decisions around its structure dominating discussions and plans for the organisation that would become the United Nations. The sponsoring nations wished to create a structure within which they were free and able to respond to any possible threats in a manner of their choosing, without having an obligation to respond to threats of lesser importance to them (Luck 2008). They wanted to have the ability to respond to any type of international conflict peacefully or militarily where necessary, without being dragged into disputes between smaller states that they deemed unworthy of their attention or military expense. The Soviet Union, in particular, wanted to create a structure whereby the Security Council and, by extension, the five permanent members would dominate international peacekeeping to avoid the problems of inefficiency seen in the League of Nations (Hilderbrand 1990).

Where the League of Nations had frequently been prevented from taking action due to disagreements between states in the assembly, peacekeeping in the United Nations was to be controlled by a smaller number of states in the hope that agreement would be more likely. By appointing themselves as permanent members of the Security Council with particular privileges, the sponsoring nations designed a structure within which they could dominate decisions on intervention and military action without any real sense of accountability (Luck 2008). While their position would *enable* them to act, it would not *force* them to act – they could operate a policy of selective responsibility. This permanent membership afforded to the United Kingdom, the United States, the Soviet Union, China and France was based on the recognition of their distinct role in the maintenance of international peace (Thakur 2006). Although the United Nations was framed as an international organisation, based on principles of equality, this permanent membership of the Security Council cemented the status of the major powers as more important in the maintenance of peace than any other state. It is vital that we remember that this leadership role was self-appointed, and the purpose of examining this here is to emphasise the likelihood that this structure was designed to preserve a particular global political hierarchy.

The self-appointment of permanent membership reinforces the view that these particular nations were, and continue to be, the most advanced nations in the world and encourages a Eurocentric ideology of civilisation. The role of the major powers in the Security Council simultaneously identifies them as the most advanced nations and legitimates their position in the global political hierarchy. Their permanent position as guardians of international peace and security cements their role as paternalistic educators as discussed in Patil's (2008) notion of kinship politics. The role of the permanent five members of the Security Council as the ultimate decision-making body in terms of intervention preserves the relationship between particular nations that was established through colonialism. In the face of mounting pressure to decolonise the world, these nations ensured that this new organisation would reinforce their position as responsible educators with the duty of maintaining peace internationally and intervening in conflicts within and between what they deemed less-developed nations. The structure of the Security Council is, therefore, an example of what Patil terms 'the softer kinship politics of colonial rule' (2008, 96).

POWER VERSUS RESPONSIBILITY

Claims of sovereign equality made throughout the governing documents of the United Nations are heavily undermined by the very structure of the Security Council and its development as a key organ of the United Nations, with permanent membership for particular states a fairly clear example of this. Although the initial plans for the Security Council included six non-permanent members on rotation, and despite the fact that this has been increased to ten, the ultimate authority lies with the globally powerful, and their sovereignty is protected and privileged above all else, on the understanding that they are the natural leaders of any world organisation due to their advanced position on the linear path of progress and development (Patil 2008). It is clear then that although the United Nations claims to be an international organisation based on sovereign equality, there is still a sharp hierarchical distinction in terms of which nations' sovereignty is most valid and legitimate. The power differential seen in the structure of the Security Council is of strong significance due to the procedural powers afforded to this arm of the United Nations. The Security Council is able to invoke sanctions, apply military action and make recommendations for the next secretary general, among its other roles. As such, the permanent members do dominate not only the Security Council but also, by extension, the United Nations as a whole. Although permanent membership is clearly an issue in terms of maintaining a hierarchical order of the world, what matters are the implications of this permanent membership and the powers it affords to particular states. Chapter 6 will explore this in more detail, looking at selectivity in terms of military intervention in order to illustrate the ongoing significance of permanent membership within the Security Council. Here, however, it is necessary to outline the underlying structures that have been established in order to allow for that selectivity. The key aspect with regards to the dominance of the permanent members of the Security Council and the powers afforded to them is the principle of unanimity between the permanent members and their ability to veto. This issue was one that threatened the very establishment United Nations as an organisation, as chapter 1 briefly touched upon.

The Charter of the United Nations states in Article 27 that decisions on non procedural matters within the Security Council

> shall be made by an affirmative vote of nine members including the concurring votes of the permanent members; provided that, in decisions under Chapter VI, and under paragraph 3 of Article 52, a party to a dispute shall abstain from voting. (United Nations 1945)

According to the Charter, decisions on security issues must have the unanimous support of the five permanent members in order to pass. These five members have the power to veto decisions and prevent a resolution from being adopted, provided that they are not directly involved in the dispute. Permanent members, therefore, have the ability to prevent action in international conflicts as part of their privileged status as international peacekeepers. In order for the United Nations to authorise the use of force, it is necessary that Britain, France, the United States, China and Russia (formerly the Soviet Union) agree that action is both justified and necessary.

The principle of abstention if a member is directly involved in a dispute is what had caused disagreement between government representatives present at Dumbarton Oaks. In fact, the proposals put forward in October 1944 state in *Section C. Voting*: 'The question of voting procedure in the Security Council is still under consideration' (United States 1944, 13). While the discussions at Dumbarton Oaks had resolved the majority of issues around the structure of the Security Council, the rules around voting procedure were unable to be resolved until the conference at San Francisco. The Soviet Union did not agree with British and American delegations that decisions around conflicts involving the major powers directly should not be voted on and, therefore, not vetoed by those involved (Hilderbrand 1990). The aim here was to prevent a situation whereby the United Nations could intervene in the affairs of the major powers, and the Soviet Union wanted to be able to prevent Security Council intervention when their own interests were directly at stake. This dispute over the power of veto, which threatened to ruin any chance of building a new international organisation, reflected a growing level of suspicion between the Soviet Union and the loose alliance between the United Kingdom and the United States, which would eventually escalate into the Cold War.

However, it was not only the major powers that were concerned about the use of veto within the Security Council. Throughout the conference in San Francisco, the Australian delegation raised concerns about the proposed power of veto within the Security Council. Dr Evatt, Australia's minister of external affairs at the time, proved to be a firm and vocal opponent of the great power privilege that was being written into the structure of the United Nations (Fox 1946). At the ninth meeting of Committee 3, which was tasked with determining the structure and procedure of the Security Council, Dr Evatt remarked:

> It seems to me to be clear that although all the parties want the Security Council to act, to make recommendations, and ten out of eleven members of the Council wish the Council to act, yet one power can say, 'No, we are not going to do it.' Such a situation is preposterous. No one could suggest any reason under such circumstances why the Security Council in such a case should be prevented from acting by the vote of one power. (Remarks of Delegate of Australia at Ninth Meeting of Committee III/1, 17 May 1945)

Australian representatives at San Francisco argued that the principle of veto and the ability of any one of the major powers to prevent action even where all other members were in agreement, showed that the Security Council and the United Nations, more broadly, had been designed in the exclusive interests of those permanent five members of the Council (Bosco 2009). The New Zealand delegation also commented upon the 'inadequate position' of smaller powers within the proposed plans for the Security Council and argued that *collective* security would not be possible if the permanent five members had the power to veto decisions (Summary Report of Fourth Meeting of Committee III/3, 10 May 1945).

If the question of decision-making and the power of veto had been contentious at Dumbarton Oaks, it was even more so at San Francisco, with various delegations representing smaller powers suggesting amendments to the proposals from Dumbarton Oaks and Yalta. Representatives from Colombia argued that the voting procedure proposed by the sponsoring governments at Dumbarton Oaks 'would put the question of peace or war in the hands of any one of the five powers' (Summary Report of 19th Meeting of Committee III/1, 12 June 1945). The Colombian delegation had already stated, however, that they were willing to support the power of veto on the provision that the autonomy of regional arrangements such as those applying to Latin America would be increased (Address by Minister of Foreign Affairs of Colombia at the Fifth Plenary Session, 30 April 1945). Despite the twenty Latin American states represented at San Francisco disagreeing on a range of issues during the conference, they maintained a united front when discussing regional defence arrangements and were supported in this by the League of Arab States (Fox 1946).

Although this structure that privileged the interests of the permanent members of the Security Council did not go unchallenged by less powerful states at the San Francisco conference, particularly by those middle powers mentioned, the ability to veto decision-making was put forward as a necessary feature of the Security Council for the permanent members, and thus a necessary feature for the United Nations as a whole to exist. Despite concerns raised by smaller states about the dominance of a minority, the cooperation of these powerful states was essential for the functioning of any international organisation. The sponsoring governments, therefore, attempted to suppress these concerns with reference to notions of *responsibility* rather than power. For example, at the sixth meeting of Committee 3, a representative of the Chinese delegation was reported to have made the following comments:

> On the question of the requirement for unanimity of the permanent members to make a vote in the Security Council effective on enforcement action, he explained it meant that there was a greater responsibility placed on their

shoulders in the arrest of aggression and in the maintenance of international peace and security. It was an important provision. He again recalled the failures of the League wherein the permanent member states had no greater responsibility than other states in this vital aspect, and pleaded for giving the new world Organization a chance. (Corrigendum to Summary Report of Sixth Meeting of Committee III/3, 14 May 1945)

As seen in the remarks made by the Chinese delegate here, the major powers frequently argued that their permanent membership was not a privilege but rather a burden. It was their responsibility or duty to ensure the success of this new organisation following the breakdown of the League of Nations and to ultimately ensure that the world was a safer place. This reliance upon the language of responsibility is powerful as a moral justification, but as many of the smaller powers present in San Francisco pointed out, this was a *selective* responsibility. Permanent members would be able to act if they wanted to but prevent action if it did not suit their interests.

This framing of the permanent five's power as responsibility was reiterated throughout the conference, largely in response to concerns made by representatives of middle powers such as Australia. Senator Connally of the US delegation made a statement that also expressed a similar sentiment:

The responsibility of the Five Permanent Members of the Security Council is momentous; it is tremendous. It may have the effect of shaking the very foundations of the earth, and I cannot conceive of anyone of the Great Powers that shall be a member of the Security Council considering lightly of that responsibility. It is our theory that they will be sensible in that sense of responsibility and that they will discharge the duties of their office not as representatives of their governments, not as representatives of their own ambitions or their own interests, but as representatives of the whole Organization in behalf of world peace and in behalf of world security. (Remarks by Senator Connally, Delegate of the United States, at the Meeting of Commission III, 20 June 1945)

Again, the power of the permanent members of the Security Council is framed as a responsibility that they are undertaking on behalf of the rest of the world. This framing of great power privilege as a responsibility rather than dominance is significant for the debates that will be explored in chapter 6 around the Responsibility to Protect. It is also, however, strongly connected to ideas around sovereignty that have been significant in the earlier chapters, whereby the concept of sovereignty within international law reinforces a particular understanding of what it means to be modern and civilised, creating a linear understanding of the progress. To frame the relationship between great powers and small powers within the United Nations as one of responsibility reproduces what Anghie terms the 'dynamic of difference', which allows one culture to be framed as universal and civilised and one as particular and uncivilised, with international law providing and legitimating mechanisms that will enable the teaching of civilisation to the uncivilised (Anghie 2005, 4). The difference is explained through the lens of development, with those nations who are deemed more advanced adopting the role or responsibility of teaching other nations how to progress.

Within the context of the Security Council, these ideas of difference as part of a continuum of development from uncivilised to civilised encourage an understanding of the permanent members as educators and responsible paternal figures, reinforcing their privilege and legitimating their dominance. The framing of the permanent members as having a distinct responsibility for all other members of the organisation allows for their decision-making to be legitimated as in the interests of international peace and security when they may, in fact, be acting less nobly in their own national interest. The fact that this notion of responsibility, and hence difference, is built into the structure of the United Nations via the Security Council highlights one of the ways in which the inequalities of formal colonialism are reproduced within international institutions. This institutionalisation of the privilege of the world's most powerful and former imperial masters within the Security Council allows for the continuation of the domination characteristic of formal colonialism. The Security Council is the foremost site of postcolonial privilege within the United Nations, where colonial dominance is institutionalised to the extent that even after decolonisation, former colonisers are able to maintain their dominance in global affairs (Krisch 2008).

The power of veto within Security Council decision-making is also the most influential structure in allowing for the issue of selectivity that is key for the arguments being made here. The great power unanimity required for the Security Council to pass and adopt a resolution means that powerful states are able to prevent action in situations where their interests are not being met; hence, the great powers have the ability to be selective about which conflicts require an international solution (Roberts and Zaum 2008). Their ability to frame their power within the Security Council not as power but as responsibility legitimates their decision-making as acting in the interests of humanity, whereas in reality, the major powers have the capacity to act in their own interests and prevent action that would have negative consequences for their individual political relationships (Murray 2012).

SACRIFICING SOVEREIGNTY

The notion of sovereignty is of prime importance within the context of the Security Council, particularly with regard to intervention. The Charter of the United Nations states in Article 1: 'Nothing contained within the present Charter shall authorize the United Nations to intervene in matters which are essentially within the domestic jurisdiction of any state' (United Nations 1945, 3). However, the process of Security Council intervention appears to be in contradiction with this, especially when we consider the role of the five permanent members of the Security Council in this decision-making process. When members of the Security Council seek to intervene in the affairs of another country, breaching traditional understandings of sovereignty, hierarchical orders of power, interest and ideology affect the decision-making process (Jones 2013). The struggle in terms of sovereign equality in these contexts becomes one between smaller states and the world's most powerful states, which is a struggle that it is impossible for smaller states to win. Within the broader structures of the United Nations, all member states have the opportunity to participate in discussions as independent sovereigns. The General Assembly provides the space within which these discussions are most able to happen (United Nations 1945). What the structure of the Security Council requires is that smaller states relinquish their rights as sovereigns and allow decisions to be made on their behalf with regard to acts of aggression and subsequent interventions (military or otherwise). For the Security Council, the aim has never been equality in terms of representation but rather unity and control in decision-making (Luck 2008). This surrender of sovereignty did not go unrecognised by those present at the birth of the organisation, and concerns were raised around the role of the permanent members of the Security Council and the level of power afforded to them by the structure of the organisation, as seen previously in the remarks made by the delegates of Australia and New Zealand.

Concerns around this sacrifice were raised at the conference in San Francisco and continued throughout the early years of the organisation. After the ratification of the Charter at San Francisco in 1945, Dr Zuleta Angel of Colombia chaired the first plenary meeting of the General Assembly in 1946 and highlighted the issues around sovereignty in his opening statement:

> The five great Powers which, by virtue of Articles 24 and 27 of the Charter, and by the very nature of things, will shoulder the chief responsibility for the maintenance of peace and security, will bring not only the immense power of their military, financial and industrial resources, but something more important, without which their very power would be nothing but the prelude to an unthinkable cataclysm; I mean good will, divested of every shred of intrigue or

trickery, and that spirit of co-operation which is vital in order to maintain among them of good understanding upon which our whole Organization rests. In signing the Charter, the other Powers have already deposited as their first contribution to this great undertaking, a large part of that which they hold most dear and most precious, a large part, that is, of their sovereignty. They made this sacrifice with deep emotion, but without hesitation, in the belief that here was the beginning of a new era in which their security would be collectively guaranteed by adequate and effective means, and any aggression or attempt at aggression directed against them would be severely repressed. (United Nations General Assembly 1946, 38)

There was a recognition that smaller member states of the United Nations were sacrificing their own sovereignty in order to support the structure of the organisation and the role of the Security Council as the sponsors envisaged it. As noted previously, without the Security Council on the terms outlined by the representatives at Dumbarton Oaks, there would be no United Nations at all. However, this recognition highlights once again the way in which claims to sovereign equality made in the Charter stood in contradiction to the very structure of the United Nations from the outset. For the organisation to exist, it was necessary for the sovereignty of some states to be privileged and the sovereignty of other states to be sacrificed.

The way in which this sacrifice of sovereignty is framed is also significant in that it is based on the understanding that the major powers are 'by the very nature of things' the most advanced nations and, therefore, the most qualified to shoulder the responsibility of maintaining international peace and security. This draws upon racialised ideas of what it means to be modern, whereby non-European states were culturally and politically 'immature' (Grovogui 1996). Rather than understanding the structure of the Security Council as a reinforcement of hierarchical global positioning and the power of the permanent members as a new form of colonial management, even those smaller states that had highlighted concerns around the dominance of the major powers were complicit in the maintenance of a discourse of development and progress. The status, position and 'responsibility' of the major powers are naturalised, and their role in the organisation is legitimated through an understanding of the world that equates cultural difference with the notion of development and civilisation. They are part of maintaining what Anghie terms the 'dynamic of difference' (2005, 4).

In what might sceptically be seen as an attempt to distract attention away from this issue of sovereign equality within the structures of the Security Council, the representatives at Dumbarton Oaks had also included proposals for a General Assembly, which would provide a space for all member states to discuss issues of international cooperation. The General Assembly was to be made up of representatives from every member state, and should have the right to consider the general principles of cooperation in the maintenance of international peace and security, including the principles governing disarmament and the regulation of armaments; to discuss any questions relating to the maintenance of international peace and security brought before it by any member or members of the Organization or by the Security Council; and to make recommendations with regard to any such principles or questions. (United States 1944, 10)

The General Assembly would be a space for each member state, large or small, to have their voice heard on broad issues to be considered by the United Nations. Crucially, however, the proposals specified that the General Assembly did not have the right to make recommendations on its own initiative 'on any matter relating to the maintenance of international peace and security which is being dealt with by the Security Council' (United States 1944, 10). In theory, the General Assembly would form a space where all member states could have their say on matters of international peace and security, but in practice, once a conflict was being dealt with by the Security Council, the General Assembly was not permitted to make any recommendations. Control over appropriate action was to remain in the hands of the major powers, with their ability to veto suggested responses. The General Assembly, in this sense, was designed to placate smaller nations, giving them a space within which to vent their opinions and attempt to address the principle of sovereign equality (Hilderbrand 1990, 108).

These initial contradictions in terms of sovereignty and sovereign equality, particularly in relation to the structures of the organisation and the Security Council, allowed for the development of an organisation that rearticulated the power of the most powerful and set up structures that would later allow for a redefinition of ideas of sovereignty that legitimates this power further. In more recent years, and particularly since the 1990s, the United Nations has arguably attempted to address issues of selectivity within the Security Council, and details of these changes in policy over time will be outlined in chapter 6. In spite of this, the issues of power politics and the dominance of the permanent five members of the Security Council continue to result in the selective application of United Nations policy.

FROM MANDATES TO TRUSTEESHIP

The United Nations Conference on International Organisation (UNCIO) in San Francisco, in theory, provided a space for all those invited as potential members of the United Nations to discuss the proposals made by the sponsoring governments at Dumbarton Oaks and to agree on the contents of what would become the Charter of the United Nations. As such, issues of sovereignty and trusteeship inevitably featured in the discussions. However, in reality, despite the sponsoring nations framing the San Francisco conference as a space for all nations to play a part in developing a universal organisation, discussions on working papers were limited in the same way that discussions on decolonisation were limited and did not allow for any significant modifications by smaller states (Twitchett 1969). San Francisco was, in reality, a space for prospective member states to agree to the proposals generated by the sponsoring nations at Dumbarton Oaks. This final section of this chapter will highlight the ways in which discussions around the trusteeship at San Francisco were centred on a problematic ideology of development and failed to deal with the contradictory nature of a system of trusteeship and a commitment to sovereign equality.

Organisationally, the conference was divided into four commissions: Commission I, General Provisions; Commission II, General Assembly; Commission III, Security Council; and Commission IV, International Court of Justice (United Nations 2019). Each commission was then subdivided, resulting in twelve committees in total, each with a different focus in terms of establishing an agreed Charter. Committee 4 of Commission II was tasked with dealing with the existing mandate territories left over from the League's days and developing a system of trusteeship that would address the requirements of the relationship between dependent territories and their sovereign administrators. In spite of the range of perspectives held by committee members, the outcomes were largely in line with the wishes of the imperial powers. On the issue of trusteeship, even amendments suggested by some of the major powers at Dumbarton Oaks – namely the Soviet Union and China – were only tentatively included in final drafts. Existing imperial powers did not see independence as a normal outcome of colonial status and, as such, were unwilling to include independence as the key outcome of a system of trusteeship (Gilchrist 1945). Sovereignty for colonial territories was not considered to be a priority for discussion at the San Francisco conference. Rather, the imperial powers that dominated the conference sought to maintain a system of control by transferring colonial territories from the controversial League of Nations mandate system to a seemingly new, although in-reality-not-much-different, United Nations Trusteeship System. They sought to minimise the discussion of decolonisation despite mounting public pressure.

Concerns around the idea of independence as an objective of this proposed system within the committee meetings came largely from the delegation of the United Kingdom. Minutes from the fourth meeting of this committee state that the representative of the United Kingdom 'warned the Committee against confusing independence with liberty. What the dependent people wanted was an increasing measure of self-government; independence would come, if at all, by natural development' (Summary of Fourth Meeting of Committee

II/4, 14 May 1945). The delegation of the United Kingdom was keen to prevent independence from being written into the Charter as the necessary eventual outcome of trusteeship. This quote exemplifies this British attitude to dependent territories and emphasises the strong belief in the notion of progress as linear and the idea that particular nations exist in a 'time-lag' (Bhabha 1994). Dependent territories are framed as being in an earlier stage of development, as being earlier versions of European states, with an understanding that they would progress naturally and eventually be qualified to be recognised as independent sovereigns, while all the time emphasising their dependence. Although this progression is framed as natural, their development had become the responsibility of those sovereign states that had achieved civilisation, and, hence, for the delegation of the United Kingdom, the purpose of the trusteeship system was to allow for the continuation of colonial rule that may or may not result in independence.

British representatives at San Francisco clearly sought to protect the empire and minimise United Nations support for independence for colonies and former League of Nations mandate territories. Prior to San Francisco, British prime minister Winston Churchill had been assured by the other sponsoring nations at Yalta that no colony of the British Empire would be subject to the United Nations system of control without British consent (Baehr and Gordenker 2005). Despite assurances that the United Nations system would be voluntary for those colonies that were not either mandate territories or former colonies of enemy states after the Second World War, the British delegation seemed keen to prevent independence becoming a compulsory eventual target. However, the principle of independence for colonial territories was significant for the representatives of the Soviet Union, who had also raised the issue of trusteeship at Dumbarton Oaks (Haas 2009). In the same meeting of Committee 4, minutes state that:

> The Delegate from the Soviet Union observed that every member of the United Nations would be responsible for the system to be established. He did not agree that self-government alone would be an adequate objective, but emphasized the importance of independence, and reminded the Committee that the amendments to the Dumbarton Oaks draft proposed by the four sponsoring governments included 'the self-determination of peoples' among the aims of the United Nations; this principle could hardly be omitted from the trusteeship chapter. (Summary of Fourth Meeting of Committee II/4, 14 May 1945)

The delegation for the Soviet Union was clearly keen to challenge the aspects of the United Nations that would continue to legitimate imperial rule in any form.

Indeed, the representatives of the Soviet Union expressed increasingly anti-colonial sentiments throughout the course of the conference as their relationship with the other sponsoring nations became progressively tense. Relations, particularly between the Soviets and the Americans, began to deteriorate, resulting in a Soviet desire to increase their anti-colonial objections in order to present themselves as the singular proponents of true democracy (Anderson 2003). Their difficult relationship with the existing colonial powers led to an increased focus on supporting independence as the ultimate objective for colonial and former mandate territories under the new United Nations system. This view was reinforced in the Soviet amendments to the US draft on the trusteeship system, which proposed that the basic objectives of the trusteeship system should include the promotion of

> the political, economic, and social advancement of the trust territories and their inhabitants and their progressive development towards self-government and self-determination with active participation of peoples of these territories having the aim to expedite the achievement by them of the full national independence. (Amendments of the Soviet Delegation to the United States Draft on Trusteeship System, 11 May 1945)

In contrast to the British view that independence would be an eventual natural outcome for some (but not all) of the territories under the new trusteeship system, for the Soviets, the trusteeship system needed to have much clearer aims in terms of decolonisation and the full independence of dependent territories. For them, it was important that independence be written into the Charter rather than being left as a decision to be made by administering nations and colonial powers. The independence of all territories was a necessary condition for the United Nations to fulfil its commitment to sovereign equality.

While the histories of the United Nations emphasise its desire to distance itself from the League of Nations and stress its novelty as an institution, the issue of trusteeship within the United Nations demonstrates the continuation of the strategies of colonial management seen in the League of Nations mandate system, as well as the continuation of problematic underlying discourses of development and civilisation. The understanding that sovereign equality in the United Nations was a move away from the imperialist understandings of sovereignty in the League of Nations, therefore, seems incorrect. Rather, what we find is a contradiction between the claims to equality made in the Charter and the systems it details. The very fact that the United Nations developed such a system for the management of territories and that independence was not always to be considered appropriate as a progressive development seems incongruent with its claims to 'the equal rights of men and women and of nations large and small' as outlined in the preamble to the Charter (United Nations 1945). Therefore, we must look more critically at the idea of sovereignty itself in international law and how it allows a particular understanding of the progress.

To recap, the idea of sovereignty in international law is guilty of neglecting to recognise its European origins and aiming to downplay its relationship to colonialism. International law is considered universally applicable, based on the interaction of sovereign states. However, the concept of sovereignty which features in international law is European in origin, raising an ideological conflict between its proposed universality and the denial of sovereignty to non-Europeans through the historical process of colonialism. Understanding the European origins of sovereignty as a concept allows us to see its role in the colonial 'civilising mission', whereby the colonial powers saw themselves as 'redeeming the backward, aberrant, violent, oppressed, undeveloped people of the non-European world by incorporating them into the universal civilization of Europe' (Anghie 2005, 3). What this does is create what Anghie terms the 'dynamic of difference', whereby a gap is created between two cultures with one as 'universal' (i.e. civilised) and one as 'particular' (i.e. uncivilised) (2005, 4). This 'dynamic of difference' allows colonialism to be justified as a process of civilising the uncivilised and incorporating 'backwards' nations into a stable system of international law.

This ideology is apparent in the discussions around the Trusteeship System at San Francisco, particularly in remarks made by British delegate Lord Cranborne. During a speech at the third meeting of Commission II (General Assembly), Lord Cranborne stressed the British expertise in matters of colonialism and argued for the necessity of non-specific principles on matters of trusteeship by saying that:

> It is sometimes imagined by those who have not very closely studied colonial policy that all Colonies are alike. That is very far from the truth. They differ as much from each other as do metropolitan territories. They range from the most primitive areas in the Pacific and Central Africa to such highly civilized countries as Ceylon, Malta and Java. They are inhabited by peoples of different races, peoples of different religions and peoples at different stages of civilisation. Each must be administered differently to take account of the varying traditions, culture and capacities of the indigenous people. (Corrigendum to Verbatim Minutes of Third Meeting of Commission II, 20 June 1945)

Lord Cranborne's speech again emphasises this dichotomy between civilised and uncivilised, perpetuating the understanding that people in particular parts of the world are naturally endowed with an advanced level of social complexity, while other nations are savage or barbarous (Tarazona 2012).

This ideology fails to account for how it is that some countries come to be 'advanced' while others remain 'backwards' or 'primitive'. Colonialism is seen as the solution rather than the problem.

Within the context of international law, sovereignty is then born out of this encounter. The civilised nations are sovereign and the uncivilised must be instructed on how to be civilised in order to become sovereign. However, where European sovereignty was constructed as natural by international law, former colonies had to be granted sovereignty based on their adherence to European notions of civilisation (Grovogui 1996). Within the context of the United Nations, this sovereignty would be granted to particular territories, although not necessarily all territories, through the trusteeship system, which saw the creation of new forms of domination and control administered by colonial powers via the United Nations as an international institution. These new forms of control were justified by presenting colonialism, as Lord Cranborne does, as a process of civilisation and development. The generally accepted understanding of international law as universal, however, disguises the colonial history of the concept of sovereignty and reproduces the 'dynamic of difference', legitimising inequalities in the global system (Anghie 2005).

This leads us to a rather more different understanding of sovereignty than the one presented by the United Nations. If we see sovereignty not as preceding colonialism but being created *through the process* of colonialism, it is not an unbiased way of understanding international relations. While international law is theoretically based on sovereign equality between states, we have already seen in chapter 2 that international institutions created two distinct models of sovereignty: European sovereignty and non-European sovereignty (see, for example, Parfitt 2011 on Ethiopia). This is the only way in which it is possible to understand the coexistence of international law and colonialism. If we understand this to be true, it becomes clear that sovereignty is not a uniform category. The norms by which a state is considered to be sovereign are subject to change depending on the context (Doty 1996). The fact that definitions of sovereignty are historically, socially and politically contingent, therefore, suggests a challenge to the ideological universality of international law and, thus, a challenge to the equality of institutions with sovereignty as their basis, such as the United Nations.

Examining documents from the discussions around trusteeship in San Francisco provides an insight into the determination of the major powers to prevent the realisation of commitments to sovereign equality. The trusteeship system was designed to legitimise inequality through the concept of sovereignty, with colonies and dependent territories being excluded from equality as a result of their inability to be sovereign. Having explored the structure of the system of trusteeship within the United Nations and the discussions held around it in San Francisco, it is possible to take issue with the United Nations' commitment to sovereign equality. This chapter has shown, through the use of archival data, the way in which the system of trusteeship established by the United Nations was not underpinned by a belief in the equality of all nations but rather that it was based upon a hierarchical ordering of society and problematic ideologies of development and civilisation. Even in the face of opposition from the Soviet Union – a key player in the establishment of the United Nations – the delegation of the United Kingdom was able to argue for a system that protected the sovereign right of the British Empire to rule over its territories over the right of its territories to be sovereign and equal.

It is worth noting, at this point, the complexities of framing the Security Council in terms of postcolonial privilege and neocolonial power. The inclusion of the Soviet Union and China within this understanding of the United Nations – and the Security Council more specifically – seems somewhat contradictory. However, the purpose of this chapter is not to account for the full nature of the Security Council in postcolonial terms but to argue that colonialism was key to the formation of the United Nations as an institution. While the inclusion of powers that were encouraging decolonisation might seem to suggest that the United Nations was abandoning colonialism as a global structure, as will be discussed in further detail, the inclusion of France was a British assertion to maintain support for empire. Thus, while the Soviet Union and China cannot be viewed as imperial powers in the same sense as Britain or France, they are nonetheless a part of an institution that has its roots in colonialism. Understanding their role in terms of the Western-centricity of the United Nations is undoubtedly complex that does require further consideration, but this goes beyond the scope of the argument being presented here and does not distract from their role in an organisation born out of colonialism.

Despite the discussions at San Francisco and the concerns and objections of the Soviet delegation, what we see in the final draft of the United Nations Charter is a hesitance to interfere in colonial relationships, with Article 76 stating that the basic objectives of the trusteeship system are

> a. to further international peace and security; b. to promote the political, economic, social and educational advancement of the inhabitants of the trust territories, and their progressive development towards self-government or independence as may be appropriate to the particular circumstances of each territory and its peoples and the freely expressed wishes of the peoples concerned, and as may be provided by the terms of each trusteeship agreement. (United Nations 1945)

The final draft is much more reflective of the British view that independence may not be appropriate for all territories. These discourses, which are seen again here in discussions around trusteeship, construct a hierarchy that sees European civilised nations at its peak, followed by 'barbarous' nations who could be taught to be civilised and 'savages' who were entirely unable to achieve the levels of social complexity belonging to Europeans (Tarazona 2012, 917). This desire to construct the world in terms of civilised/uncivilised and backwards/advanced is as present in the rhetoric of the United Nations as it was in the League of Nations, but perhaps more discretely.

This chapter has provided a re-narration of the founding of the United Nations at San Francisco, highlighting the continuities of the League of Nations and challenging the narrative of rupture. In doing so, it has established the centrality of colonial power dynamics within the structures of the United Nations and reinforced the ways in which these structures enable selective responsibility. Following on from chapter 2, it has shown that the concept of sovereignty is not fixed or stable and has been used to maintain hierarchy on a global scale. The privileging of Western sovereignty over and above that of other states has been justified through a language of responsibility that draws on colonial discourses and sees universalism as a universal adherence to the European model (Grovogui 1996). Texturing these debates with archival material from anti-colonial actors both within and outside the United Nations reiterates the importance of challenging dominant narratives and providing alternative, evidenced narratives. Understanding the entrenchment of colonial power dynamics within the structures of the United Nations, particularly through principles such as sovereignty, development and responsibility, is vital in understanding how these power dynamics have been sustained following political decolonisation. The next chapter follows on chronologically to explore how these discourses enable neocolonial forms of control within the United Nations post-decolonisation.

Chapter 4

The Rise of Asia-Africa and Discourses of Development

Following the dismissal of colonial questions at San Francisco, the early years of the United Nations faced the challenge of an increased focus on the anti-colonial identity of Asia-Africa that had developed out of earlier forms of anti-imperial solidarity. This chapter traces the development of this identity at the Bandung Conference of 1955 and the ways in which its focus on solidarity through brotherhood provides resistance to established discourses of development and responsibility within the United Nations that seek to maintain a paternalism that justified colonialism and legitimised more recent neocolonial forms of control. The aim here is to develop further the theoretical understanding outlined in earlier chapters of the use of discourses of development, progress and responsibility to frame unequal global power relations as natural while also foregrounding the ways in which this has been resisted historically.

While the established narrative frames decolonisation as a moral decision on the part of the major powers within the United Nations, this chapter explores archival material that points to the complex political environment of the Cold War and the ways that this was utilised by the solidarity movement of Asia-Africa. It considers the significance of such solidarities in challenging dominant discourses within international relations and providing inspiration for continued forms of resistance. Reading decolonisation as an inevitable response to the demands made by colonised and formerly colonised states and their allies rather than as a benevolent gesture on behalf of the West shifts our understanding of the role of the major powers and disrupts the narrative that decolonisation was a part of the United Nations' progressive aims and ideals. It acknowledges that decolonisation was achieved *in spite* of the wishes of the major powers, not because of them. This, in turn, provides a more critical understanding of how responsibility functions within the United Nations and the persistence of hierarchical understandings of sovereignty that enable selective responsibility.

DISCOURSES OF DEVELOPMENT

As chapter 3 outlined, the United Nations trusteeship system is grounded in a discourse of development that supports Eurocentric understandings of what it means to be civilised, whereby Europe is considered the height of development or civilisation. This discourse of development that was important in the implementation of colonial rule has been consistently reproduced throughout the history of the United Nations and within the League of Nations before it through the mandate system. Both systems have framed the major powers as acting in the role of paternalistic educators of the uncivilised and have enabled neocolonial technologies of management through an understanding of development that is problematic as it relies on understanding European culture as superior (Rajagopal 2003). When the formal violence and control of colonialism had been challenged, both the mandate system and the trusteeship system allowed for the maintenance of colonial power under the pretence of a more transparent form. It would be administered by an international organisation rather than individual states. In reality, relationships were still between individual states, and both systems did little to address colonial power dynamics.

In the shift from the mandate system to the trusteeship system that happened with the emergence of the United Nations, the relationship between colonies and their colonisers was accompanied by a much more explicit focus on the idea of development (Rajagopal 2003). A reminder that the aims of the trusteeship system outlined in Article 76 of the Charter include reference to

> the political, economic, social and educational advancement of the inhabitants of
> the trust territories, and their progressive development towards self-government
> or independence as may be appropriate to the particular circumstances of
> each territory and its peoples and the freely expressed wishes of the peoples
> concerned, and as may be provided by the terms of each trusteeship agreement.
> (United Nations 1945)

The aim of the system, therefore, is not independence as a fundamental principle for colonised territories but 'progressive development' towards independence, or self-government 'as may be appropriate'. Key to consider here is who sets the terms of what is considered 'progressive development' and who decides the appropriate outcome for these territories. What had previously been understood as a relationship between colonies and empires in the League of Nations was framed by the United Nations as a relationship between administering authorities and dependent territories. In response to mounting public anti-colonial pressure, the United Nations established a system that reinforced existing development discourses to legitimate problematic hierarchies built into its structure from the start. These relationships were characterised by what Patil calls 'kinship politics', framing these dependent territories as irrational and childlike, needing tutelage and guidance from the rational and paternal 'advanced' states (2008, 95). In the face of increasing anti-colonial sentiment, it was important for imperial states to establish new forms of control that could be justified as something more than domination and exploitation so that even when former colonies were granted independence, it was the result of a satisfactory adherence to the path of development established by their colonial masters (Rajagopal 2003).

For these new systems to work, it was vital that the sponsoring governments minimise discussion of the colonial question and decolonisation in the founding stages of the United Nations. As highlighted in the previous chapters, this silencing of colonialism did not only occur at the San Francisco conference in 1945; it is a silence that has been replicated and reproduced through the standard historical accounts of the emergence of the United Nations. Standard narratives of the establishment of the United Nations as an international organisation fail to acknowledge the significance of colonialism for its founding and, as a result, reproduce the problematic and inaccurate discourses of equality that surround the organisation (Getachew 2019). Chapter 3 highlighted some of the unsuccessful attempts by various groups such as the African Academy of Arts and Research and the West Indies National Council to get decolonisation and independence for the colonies onto the agenda for discussion in San Francisco, attempts that have been written out of the vast number of accounts of the history of the United Nations. The fact that these attempts made were unsuccessful and have not been included in the standard narrative tells us something significant about the United Nations. Rather than dealing with the issue of colonialism and making commitments on the subject of independence, the major powers sought to minimise discussions of this sort to enable new forms of management to be established that were not explicitly colonial but maintained the power dynamics of colonialism (see Anderson 2003; Tillery 2011; Plummer 1996).

Colonialism is also notably absent from many histories of international law and, most importantly for the arguments developed here, in accounts of the history of the concept of sovereignty. The United Nations frames sovereignty as an objective status for those states that have successfully followed European paths to development to the extent that they are able to participate in the global system, and the aim of the trusteeship system in this sense is to guide dependent territories to a level of progress where they can be granted sovereignty and participate in international relations as individual states (United Nations 1945). However, this narrative neglects the significance of colonialism for the concept of sovereignty and the development of international law more generally. The earlier chapters have shown that sovereignty as a way of governing relationships between states emerged during the colonial encounter to understand the relationship between European colonisers and their non-European colonies (Grovogui 1996; Anghie 2005). In order to justify colonial domination, imperial states were deemed sovereign and colonies were not, making international law key to the civilising mission of colonialism, with colonialism acting as the process by which uncivilised nations could become civilised and be granted sovereignty. Even where non-European or non-Western states were technically independent and recognised the version of sovereignty available to them was different and inferior (Parfitt 2011; Donaldson 2020). The United Nations' claim to be based on the sovereign equality of member states is, therefore, a contradiction in terms. These historical examples have demonstrated that in the international context, sovereignty is hierarchical and, as Krasner (2009) notes, is best understood as 'organized hypocrisy'. The perceived objectivity and universality of international law were and are defended through the idea that the status of sovereignty was attainable for all nations, and this was used to legitimate exploitation via colonialism as a civilising mission (Koskenniemi 2005).

As presented by the United Nations, sovereignty as an attainable status for all, resulting in equal participation, is a myth, yet this narrative is pervasive. Ideologies of colonialism that present Europe and the West as the end point or most advanced form of society are reproduced through a discourse of development, whereby non-Western states are seen to exist earlier (Bhabha 1994). To understand the world in terms of development and progress prioritising particular cultures and traditions over others. To challenge this is to emphasise that these discourses have enabled and justified the violence inherent in colonialism and challenge the continuation of this violence through neocolonial forms of control (Rajagopal 2003). Understanding the world in terms of development towards a singular end point will always prioritise the values of a particular culture. However, in the early years of the United Nations' existence, an alternative vision of an international community was imagined, building upon a long history of anti-colonial resistance.

THE BANDUNG CONFERENCE

After the efforts of anti-colonial activists failed to get decolonisation on the agenda in San Francisco and in the early years of the United Nations, the collective identity of Asia-Africa emerged and increased in strength. This identity was born out of an understanding that despite their religious or cultural, or even political differences, these nations were united in their suffering through shared experiences of imperial domination and exploitation and an agreement that the United Nations was not functioning as an inclusive and universal world parliament that was necessary. As such, the identity of Asia-Africa was forged through solidarity framed in terms of brotherhood and morality, in opposition to the West's identification of Asia-Africa as infantile and need of guidance (Patil 2008). As addressed in the section above, the relationship between the West and the rest of the world had historically been characterised as one of paternalism, whereas the unity of Asia-Africa was based on a strong rejection of this characterisation and solidarity through equality and brotherhood.

The Bandung Conference in April of 1955 was central to the development of this Asia-Africa identity, signifying a culmination of anti-colonial pressure on international institutions that had begun in 1927 with the League against Imperialism and launching 'an era of growing antiracist assertiveness by people of colour' (Fraser 2003, 118). It brought together twenty-nine Asian and African states and colonies at the invitation of the Indonesian president Sukarno and the Indian prime minister Jawaharlal Nehru to consolidate the demands being made of the United Nations by anti-colonial forces in terms of decolonisation and independence. Grovogui aptly describes Bandung as an estuary: 'the meetings of distinct political streams, of a historical confluence of ideas and of tidal waves of subjects and their wills' (2016, 116). Their differences notwithstanding, those present at the conference agreed on issues of economic and cultural cooperation and what the Bandung Conference ultimately represented was both a diplomatic and symbolic commitment, where Asian and African countries met to 'discuss the possible futures of the postcolonial world' (Lee 2010, 3). It signified a refusal by colonial and ex-colonial states to continue to take orders from colonisers and an acknowledgement that they could discuss international problems without the involvement of the West and provide a unified viewpoint.

The agenda proposed by the Joint Secretariat for the conference listed seven items:

1. Economic Cooperation;
2. Cultural Cooperation;
3. Problems of Dependent Peoples;
4. Racial Discrimination and Racial Problems;
5. The use of Nuclear Energy for Peaceful Purposes;
6. Weapons of Mass Destruction;
7. Promotion of World Peace and Cooperation.

('Agenda Compiled by the Joint Secretariat of the Asian-African Conference,' April 16, 1955, HPPPDA, PRC FMA 207-00015-01, 11)

In discussing economic, political and social development issues for the
states of Asia and Africa, the conference at Bandung reframed the debates.
While the United Nations had established a system that would ensure the
reproduction of colonial power dynamics by assigning administering powers
through the trusteeship system, who would 'teach' states how to develop,
discussions at Bandung were focused on the solidarities of Asia-Africa that
would encourage growth on their terms and without reliance on the West.
The archives from the Bandung Conference provide an alternative vision on
a range of international issues than those proposed by the United Nations,
which this chapter will now deal with.

Colonialism and Neocolonialism

The solidarities forged at Bandung were centred on the common experience
of colonisation and a desire to challenge the neocolonial forms of power being
established by the major imperial powers via institutions such as the United
Nations. Their unity came not from cultural or racial likenesses but from
political opposition to colonialism in any and every form (Prashad 2007).
Underpinning the conference was a spirit of anti-colonialism present in the
many speeches made and the Final Communique, which is the summary
document of the conference. The geographical location of the conference
held a deep significance for those present. In his opening speech, President
Sukarno emphasises the importance of the conference happening outside of
Europe, following a period of decolonisation for many states: 'Now we are
free, sovereign and independent. We are again masters in our own house. We
do not need to go to other continents to confer' (Sukarno 1955). Bandung
represented an important shift in the geographical location of international
politics, demonstrating that politics could happen elsewhere and without the
input of those who were, or who considered themselves to be, the world's
major powers. The majority of those nations present had been subject to
the colonial domination of Western Europe for periods spanning decades
to centuries, and so there was a strong sense of overcoming domination at
Bandung. As Wright describes it, Bandung represented a meeting of 'the
despised, the insulted, the hurt, the dispossessed – in short, the underdogs'
(1956, 12).

While reiterating the recent successes of decolonisation and independence
for some – such as India (1947), Indonesia (1947) and Sri Lanka (1948) –
Sukarno's speech goes on to describe the new guises of colonialism that the
recently independent African and Asian nations needed to be wary of:

Colonialism has also its modern dress, in the form of economic control, intellectual control, actual physical control by a small but alien community within a nation. It is a skilful and determined enemy, and it appears in many guises. It does not give up its loot easily. Wherever, whenever and however it appears, colonialism is an evil thing, and one which must be eradicated from the earth. (Sukarno 1955)

Bandung was, therefore, not solely focused on the political goal of ending the formal rule of the colonisers but on establishing new economic systems that would ensure that former colonies did not continue to be reliant upon imperial powers for survival. Bandung identified the independent state – the nation-state – as an alternative to colonialism but also as an alternative to the economic systems represented by the two opposing Cold War forces (Kanwar 2017). References to intellectual control recognise that the colonial project was not simply about the extraction of raw materials and the exploitation of labour, but it was also a cultural and ideological project. As explored in the previous section, colonialism enforced Eurocentrism and the discourses of development that would ensure that independent states would continue their relationships with the West via global capitalism. For Sukarno, a rejection of colonialism required an awareness of the myriad of ways colonisers had maintained control beyond military force and the occupation of territory and a rejection of the new 'modern' forms of colonial control.

Within the Final Communique of the conference, we also see several colonial states targeted individually in relation to situations considered urgent or of particular significance, namely the Netherlands, France and Israel. The conference 'declared its support of the rights of the people of Algeria, Morocco and Tunisia to self-determination and independence', its support of 'the rights of the Arab people of Palestine', and in the dispute between Indonesia and the Netherlands in relation to the case of West Irian (now Western New Guinea), 'urged the Netherlands government to reopen negotiations as soon as possible, to implement their obligations' (Asian-African Conference 1955). Attendees at the conference were not content to talk about colonialism only in general terms in the documents that would become public and gave their support to specific cases in the hope of pushing the international community into action.

Trade and Economic Development

The attention paid to colonial and neocolonial forms of control during the conference was to highlight a history of inequality and reinforce the extent to which this history of colonisation had impacted the economic development of states in Asia and Africa. The Final Communique identified the region's economic development as an urgent priority and provided a number of suggestions for routes to development, centred around collaboration and knowledge sharing. It states that participating countries agree to

> provide technical assistance to one another, to the maximum extent practicable, in the form of: experts, trainees, pilot projects and equipment for demonstration purposes; exchange of know-how and establishment of national, and where possible, regional training and research institutes for imparting technical knowledge and skills in cooperation with the existing international agencies. (Asian-African Conference 1955)

This commitment to knowledge sharing and assistance was sensitive to the different situations of those states present, some of whom had much more developed economies than others. Plans for trade and economic development also recognised the impact of histories of colonisation on the structure of the economies of many African states, which relied on the export of raw materials. The conference proposed that countries should diversify their exports through processing raw materials rather than exporting raw materials to be processed in Europe (Asian-African Conference 1955). This would enable states to go some way in unpicking the unequal trade relationships established through colonialism. However, in emphasising the relationship between decolonisation and development, these statements reinforce Western ideals in relation to modernisation and focus on establishing ways for former colonies to 'catch up' with the West (Chakrabarty 2010).

The desire to maintain regional control over trade and exports was unsurprising given the broader political context of the Cold War and the scepticism surrounding offers of aid by the United States. The United States was concerned about the autonomy of Asian states affecting Western influence in the region and the development of an anti-Western bloc within the United Nations, and as such, they tried to limit the participation of Asian states in the conference initially (Fraser 2003). In failing to do so, they attempted to influence the outcome of the conference in various other ways. A statement sent by the Chinese embassy in Indonesia on 25 March 1955 claims that the United States had been trying to expand foreign aid in the name of economic assistance, using a twofold strategy. Firstly, they had been recruiting Indonesian students to go and study in the United States before returning to government and civil service roles, and secondly, they had sent experts and advisors from the United States to Indonesia to observe industry and agriculture. This same statement claims that 'on the eve of the Asian-African conference; an American mail ship brought four hundred "tourists" to "tour" Indonesia' (Cable from the Chinese embassy in Indonesia, 'What the United States is Doing in Indonesia prior to the Asian-African Conference,' March 25, 1955, HPPPDA, PRC FMA

207-00002-04, 136-18). While talk of the US shipping in spies acting as tourists might seem improbable to a contemporary reader, there is no doubt that the plans being made at Bandung struck fear in the Western powers. A string of military coups followed in the 1960s, including the overthrow of Sukarno, which saw the CIA implicated (Grovogui 2016).

This tension between the United States and China at Bandung must also be contextualised within the broader international environment, whereby China had been subject to containment policies by the United States and exclusion from the United Nations (Yifeng 2017). The Chinese position at Bandung was, therefore, complex and striking a delicate balance between generating connections with African and Asian states, while abstaining from commitments to reform the United Nations where it no longer held any power. The Chinese delegation sought to explore possible trade opportunities while defending against claims of Soviet neocolonialism (Yifeng 2017). The United States, in contrast and although not present at the conference, sought to maintain a stance of non-alignment with its allies on the issue of European colonialism, while stoking anti-communist sentiment and the question of Soviet neocolonialism to contain the power of China (Fraser 2003). The divides of the Cold War infiltrated the conference and reinforced the complexities of Bandung in negotiating the competing demands and wishes of states from across the political spectrum and both sides of the Cold War divide.

Clearly, there was significant – and not unfounded – concern around the United States' interference in the Bandung Conference and the risk of regional cooperation strategies being weakened by foreign aid that would tie states to Western trade agreements. For those familiar with the development of Structural Adjustment Policies in the 1980s, the concerns over the United States' interference in the economic affairs of non-Western states are well-founded. In light of these apprehensions around money flows and the ties that come with foreign investment in industry, the Final Communique encourages the establishment of national and regional banks and insurance companies (Asian-African Conference 1955). Doing so would enable states to achieve financial cooperation outside of global institutions such as the International Monetary Fund or the World Bank. The focus of economic policies at Bandung was, therefore, independence from Western finance and increased regional cooperation that would enable newly independent states to develop their economies without being tied into inequitable trade relationships.

Cultural Cooperation

In addition to economic cooperation, a commitment to cultural cooperation was central to both the idea of the conference itself and the proposed solutions to the consequences of colonialism that the conference generated. Sukarno's opening speech speaks at length about solidarity in difference:

> We are of many different nations, we are of many different social backgrounds and cultural patterns. Our ways of life are different. Our national characters, or colours, or motifs – call it what you will – are different. Our racial stock is different, and even the colour of our skin is different. But what does that matter? Mankind is united or divided by considerations other than these. Conflict comes not from variety of skins, nor from variety of religion, but from variety of desires. All of us, I am certain, are united by more important things than those which superficially divide us. We are united, for instance, by a common detestation of colonialism in whatever form it appears. (Sukarno 1955)

This recognition of colonialism as the common enemy that unites those colonised and formerly colonised is a theme that runs through the Bandung Conference and connects it to the League against Imperialism before it. Sukarno's speech emphasises respect for differences in terms of culture, politics and religion and argues that this does not have to hinder a fight against imperialism or a broader politics of cooperation. As previously noted, relationships between states at Bandung were imagined as ties of brotherhood, of equality, rather than hierarchy. As Kamola and el-Malik (2017) argue, the anti-colonialism of this period was navigating complex relationships and involved a wide range of actors from scholars to peasants and politicians to journalists, but all were united in a common project with the shared goal of defeating their colonial masters. Where the United Nations had built an institution based on hierarchy, the solidarities at Bandung required an approach based on equitable terms of involvement. Sukarno refers to those present as 'sisters and brothers' and states that Bandung is a 'conference of brotherhood'. He goes on to describe the conference as

> a body of enlightened, tolerant opinion which seeks to impress on the world that all men and all countries have their place under the sun – to impress on the world that it is possible to live together, meet together, speak to each others, without losing one's individual identity and yet to contribute to the general understanding of matters of common concerns, and to develop a true consciousness of the interdependence of men and nations for their wellbeing and survival on earth. (Sukarno 1955)

In this speech, Sukarno provides a critique of both the United Nations and colonialism in the sense that both prioritise the voices, needs and wants of some over others. He emphasises that colonialism required, or indeed forced, the loss of individual identity for many.

The Final Communique reflects this critique in stating that 'the existence of colonialism in many parts of Asia and Africa in whatever form it may be not only prevents cultural cooperation but also suppresses the national cultures of the people' (Asian-African Conference 1955). For colonialism to maintain control, it has to create structures of dependency that prevent cultural cooperation and discourage national culture by deeming it 'uncivilised'. The reference here to colonialism 'in whatever form it may be' reinforces the idea that national culture is not easily reestablished following decolonisation as 'civilised' culture comes to be understood as synonymous with white European culture (Fanon 1967). Colonialism functions by establishing European values as universal values, and those are values of reason, individualism and scepticism (particularly where religion is concerned). As such, the battle being fought at Bandung was to establish means of cooperation that would reclaim national cultures, to work together in spite of the differences that might divide states. The Final Communique argues that embracing a tradition of tolerance in Asian and African cultural cooperation would provide a blueprint for a broader global cooperation (Asian-African Conference 1955).

War

The threat of nuclear war between the United States and the Soviet Union loomed heavy at Bandung, and so there are a significant number of references to this in archival documents. On 22 April 1955, the then prime minister of India, Jawaharlal Nehru, made a speech entitled 'World Peace and Cooperation'. In it, he talks about the very real prospect of a Third World War that would 'bring us not only to the abyss of civilisation and culture but would mean total destruction' (Nehru 1955). For Nehru, a commitment to non-alignment with either side during the Cold War was essential to preventing this. He saw the role of those present at Bandung as a mediating force:

> Every step that takes place in reducing that area in the world which may be called the 'unaligned area' is a dangerous step and leads to war. It reduces that objectivity, that balance, that outlook which other countries without military might can perhaps exercise. (Nehru 1955)

For Nehru, non-alignment was the responsibility of the Asian-African alliance in order to prevent a Third World War that looked set to be even more dangerous than the previous two. Similarly, Sukarno's opening address calls upon those present at Bandung to fight for peace:

> We, the peoples of Asia and Africa, 1,400,000,000 strong, far more than half the human population of the world, we can mobilise what I have called the Moral

Violence of Nations in favour of peace. We can demonstrate to the minority
of the world which lives on the other continents that we, the majority, are for
peace, not for war, and that whatever strength we have will always be thrown
on to the side of peace. (Sukarno 1955)

This position was frequently articulated throughout the conference,
particularly with regard to aspects of military defence. While it was accepted
that states had the right to self-defence in response to military aggression,
there was an agreement to refrain from the collective defence that served
the interests of the major powers (Acharya and Tan 2008). These nations
would no longer play the role of protection for their imperial masters. Their
identity would now be defined by their role in an Asia-Africa alliance, no
longer by the colonised-coloniser relationship. The Final Communique
reflects this pledge to non-alignment and harness nuclear energy for 'peaceful
purposes' rather than war (Asian-African Conference 1955). It states that the
conference agreed that 'disarmament and the prohibition of the production,
experimentation and use of nuclear and thermonuclear weapons of war are
imperative to save mankind and civilization from the fear and prospect of
wholesale destruction' (Asian-African Conference 1955).

In his speech, Nehru also warned against the organisation of military
blocs and pacts, arguing that they lead to a false sense of security. Speaking
specifically about NATO, Nehru stated explicitly that 'NATO today is one
of the most powerful protectors of colonialism' (Nehru 1955). He gives the
example of Goa to illustrate this:

Here is the little territory of Goa, in India, which Portugal holds. We get letters
from the NATO powers – mind you, Portugal is a member of NATO – and
Portugal has approached its fellow members in the NATO on this point – telling
us, 'You should not do anything in regard to Goa, you should not do this and
that'. (Nehru 1955)

While there was agreement on the need for disarmament and to prevent the
production of nuclear weapons, Nehru was reluctant to formalise any military
alliances and indeed to support those already in existence. Fundamentally,
the Bandung Conference argued for disarmament and peace, calling upon
the United Nations to address this as a matter of urgency (Asian-African
Conference 1955).

Reaffirming the Principles of the United Nations

As well as being a space for creating a unified Asia-Africa identity outside
of the United Nations, the conference aimed to establish a cohesive set of

proposals for anti-colonial resistance *within* the United Nations. In returning to the United Nations with demands for independence, those present at the Bandung Conference needed to be clear and united in their approach. The conference succeeded in generating a well-defined set of proposals, with the Final Communique stating the following agreements:

> The Conference is agreed: (a) in declaring that colonialism in all its manifestations is an evil which should speedily be brought to an end; (b) in affirming that the subjection of peoples to alien subjugation, domination and exploitation constitutes a denial of fundamental human rights, is contrary to the Charter of the United Nations and is an impediment to the promotion of world peace and cooperation; (c) in declaring its support of the cause of freedom and independence for all such peoples, and (d) in calling upon the powers concerned to grant freedom and independence to such peoples. (Asian-African Conference 1955)

This statement emphasises the contradictions apparent in the Charter, particularly in relation to colonialism as a violation of human rights formalised in 1947. The conference resolved that an organisation committed to protecting human rights and the promoting world peace could not also support the continued existence of colonialism in any form and for any territory.

A summary of talks between Premier Zhou of China and Nehru shows that China was keen to establish a permanent institution after the Bandung Conference that would 'facilitate contact between the governments from the participating countries, especially since some of the participating countries of the conference were not UN members' (Summary of the Talks between Premier Zhou and Nehru and U Nu, April 16, 1955, HPPPDA, PRC FMA 207-00015-01, 1-10). This institution was envisaged as a space for liaison rather than an organisation that would require binding agreements on the part of its members; however, Nehru 'doubted that such an institution could be effective and said that it was not wise if the conference did anything to enter into a rivalry with the UN' (Summary of the Talks between Premier Zhou and Nehru and U Nu, April 16, 1955, HPPPDA, PRC FMA 207-00015-01, 1-10). While the conference was, in part, born out of dissatisfaction with the United Nations, archival documents suggest that participants still held out hope that reform was possible and that there was a lack of desire to develop a separate formal organisation. The aim here was not to replicate the United Nations but to create spaces for discussion and collaboration that could facilitate economic development without the United Nations and seek to reform the organisation from within.

This belief in reform is evident in the Final Communique, which highlights several contradictions and false promises made by the United Nations, calling for implementing the principles stated in the Charter. For example, in the context of points on cultural cooperation, it states that the policies of colonialism that had denied people the ability to study their language and culture amount to 'a denial of the fundamental rights of man, impede cultural advancement in this region and also hamper cultural cooperation on the wider international plane' (Asian-African Conference 1955). The Final Communique uses the language of human rights that the United Nations had proclaimed in 1947 to challenge the ongoing consequences of colonisation and neocolonialism. It goes on to say

> the Conference declared its full support of the principle of self-determination of peoples and nations as set forth in the Charter of the United Nations and took note of the United Nations resolutions on the rights of peoples and nations to self-determination, which is a pre-requisite of the full enjoyment of all fundamental Human Rights. (Asian-African Conference 1955)

With anti-colonialism at the heart of the Conference, the Final Communique of Bandung uses the principles of the Charter of the United Nations in order to fight for the rights of those still colonised by making clear the contradiction of having self-determination as a primary principle while legitimising the continuation of colonial rule.

The Final Communique argues that in order for the United Nations to be effective, membership must be universal and calls upon the Security Council to support the admission of those countries that qualified: 'Cambodia, Ceylon, Japan, Jordan, Libya, Nepal, a unified Vietnam' (Asian-African Conference 1955). It also goes on to critique the structure of the Security Council, stating that:

> The Conference considered that the representation of the countries of the Asian African region on the Security Council, in relation to the principle of equitable geographical distribution, was inadequate. It expressed the view that as regards the distribution of the non-permanent seats, the Asian-African countries which, under the arrangement arrived at in London in 1946, are precluded from being elected, should be enabled to serve on the Security Council, so that they might make a more effective contribution to the maintenance of international peace and security. (Asian-African Conference 1955)

As was the case in San Francisco, there was concern over the dominance of Western powers within the Security Council, which plays such a powerful role in United Nations politics, particularly with regard to intervention and the maintenance of peace. For those present at Bandung, the maintenance of international peace and security required participation on more equitable terms that would counterbalance the weight of the West.

While reform of the systems within the United Nations was deemed important, the primary request from Bandung to the United Nations was freedom. Where the trusteeship system of the United Nations encouraged 'development,' which this chapter has argued was a revised form of colonial control, the Bandung Conference tied the maintenance of international peace to freedom for all those who were still considered dependent peoples. This was grounded in a belief that 'all nations should have the right to freely choose their own political and economic systems and their own way of life, in conformity with the purposes and principles of the Charter of the United Nations' (Asian-African Conference 1955). While the major powers wanted to establish a path to independence that would require conformity with Western political and economic systems, those present at Bandung reinforced the notion that freedom and self-determination necessitated that each state had the freedom to choose their own political, economic and cultural systems. Anything less than this amounted to a continuation of colonialism.

Unsurprisingly, the archives reveal a variety of reactions to the Conference on the whole and to the Final Communique in particular. The Chinese Foreign Ministry compiled a report of 'Comments on the Asian-African Conference from Capitalist Ruled Countries After the Asian-African Conference' wherein United States diplomat Allen Dulles had said that he was 'greatly inspired after reading the communique as the conference placed a high hope on and had confidence in UN' (Report from the Chinese Foreign Ministry, 'Comments on the Asian-African Conference from Capitalist Ruled Countries After the Asian-African Conference' May 10, 1955, HPPPDA, PRC FMA 207-00059-01). However, the reaction from French representatives was less positive, with outrage that the conference had discussed the case of Algeria. Criticism of France at the conference had been anticipated by the French Press, as demonstrated by an article in Le Figaro from 18 April, which reads:

> Although politically divided, the states represented in Bandung are, however, much closer in their desire to put an end to the domination of the white man. Does this mean that the white nations will be in the dock? It looks certain that many acrimonious anti-colonial declarations will be heard. Some Arab states, including Libya, which claims to speak on behalf of the Tunisians, Algerians and Moroccans, will surely denounce France. Others will criticise the United Kingdom. In general, when the conference participants speak to the outside world, they will make a show of defying those countries that expect to continue their world domination despite the fact that they represent scarcely one fifth of the world's population. (Massip 1955, 2)

Clearly, a conference that set out to discuss colonialism and the situation of dependent territories was not an entirely welcome event for those who had economic and political investments in maintaining the status quo. However, the commitment to working within the United Nations to reform existing systems seemed to suggest a less dramatic shift than first anticipated. The states present at Bandung acknowledged the legitimacy of the United Nations while requesting a greater voice (Vitalis 2013). This commitment to reform has continued in various forms since 1955, which will be outlined in the next chapter.

BANDUNG AND THE COLD WAR

Within the United Nations, the spirit of the statements made at Bandung proved to be a powerful moment in disrupting global politics as they had existed until that point. The Cold War provided a moment of opportunity, both for the anti-colonial movement and the two superpowers. The struggle against colonialism within the United Nations had become a major issue of ideology, and the Soviet Union quickly realised they could use this to their advantage, claiming to be the 'true defenders' of freedom among those major powers that continued to defend colonial rule (Mazower 2012, 249). The anti-colonial movement, therefore, found itself with a key ally in the form of the Soviet Union, which sought to establish influence over the states of Asia-Africa in their expansion of the socialist project. This Soviet anti-colonial approach, in fact, has a longer history than this particular moment in that their critique of capitalism as Western exploitation had contributed towards an increased level of self-awareness among colonised states (Mamlyuk 2017). The United States, on the other hand, while also seeking to establish influence and harvest support during the Cold War era, was disadvantaged by its close relationship with European colonial powers. Despite its public anti-colonial stance, the United States was reluctant to openly confront its closest allies over the issue of colonialism (Fraser 2003). The major powers were locked in conflict, with the Security Council being rendered almost useless due to the extraordinary use of veto during decision-making, and so much of this played out in the General Assembly. As all member states have a seat in the General Assembly, this became the central site for anti-colonial resistance by the newly formed Asia-Africa alliance, bolstered by the support of the Soviet Union. This period, therefore, saw the General Assembly become a key space within which newly independent states could push decolonisation onto the agenda, confronting and challenging the power of their former colonisers (Patil 2008).

In addition to the political consequences of Bandung, in the form of addressing decolonisation within the United Nations, it also represented a significant moment in terms of non-Western solidarity. Indeed, one of the key agreements of the conference was that regardless of the ideological divide between nations within the context of the Cold War, conflicting political beliefs or ideologies should not be the basis for excluding nations from international forms of solidarity (Acharya and Tan 2008). While nations had differing positions on the ideological divide of capitalism versus socialism, this was not considered as grounds to prevent the development of anti-colonial solidarity. Bandung signified an understanding of international cooperation as acceptance of diversity and an agreement to overcome ideological conflicts in the interests of pursuing rights for the colonised and formerly colonised (Acharya and Tan 2008). Regardless of the differing political positions of those in attendance, the core message of Bandung was the rejection of colonialism in all its forms.

The anti-colonial resistance to the United Nations that had taken shape during the San Francisco conference reached its peak at the Bandung conference of 1955. The failure of the United Nations to deal with colonialism and formalise a commitment to independence in 1945 generated an intense resistance to the organisation and forged an alliance between a large number of Asian and African states. The Bandung conference, alongside meetings that followed, had provided the space within which the Asia-Africa alliance could prepare the demands that became associated with the Third World Project, which included a redistribution of global resources, a fairer global labour market and a recognition of the contribution of Asia and Africa to developments in technology and culture (Prashad 2007). It was a key moment in a longer-term project that sought to address global inequality, beginning with demands for full independence for the world's remaining colonies. The Third World alliance was eventually given its opportunity to push decolonisation onto the agenda as part of the years of Cold War conflict that threatened to render the United Nations irrelevant and incompetent due to the prevention of action by the United States and the Soviet Union. Eventually, this anti-colonial pressure was too huge to ignore, and the United Nations had to address decolonisation.

THE POWER OF BANDUNG

In the outcome of the Bandung Conference, we see a clear, unified demand for decolonisation in every sense and a growing scepticism of the United Nations and the institutionalised privilege of the world's major powers. The Final Communique shows an acknowledgement of the contradictions inherent in the Charter, which enshrines the principle of human rights while allowing the continuation of imperial domination via trusteeship. To bring this chapter back to its beginning, the significance of Bandung is not only that it represented an agreement to cooperation but that it also provided a clear and public critique of the Eurocentrism of the United Nations. Where the trusteeship system frames underdevelopment as a natural problem that needed to be addressed through supervision and progression towards European cultural values, Bandung reframes these problems and places colonialism at the centre. It provides an alternative vision for economic growth that requires the rejection of colonial power structures and the reclaiming of non-Western culture as valuable. It highlights the dangers of an unequal distribution of power and resources globally in its warnings of a Third World War and provided an important critique of global institutions such as the United Nations, hierarchically organised around this unequal distribution of global power. While we might think critically about the conference's commitment to modernisation as the goal for states post-decolonisation, the strategies and commitments outlined at Bandung provide a strong challenge to the rhetoric of responsibility within the United Nations and highlight its contradictions. Instead, these strategies would see former colonies take responsibility for their own economic, political and social development. Examining the debates at Bandung provides a powerful critique of the discourses that establish and legitimate great power privilege within the United Nations, enabling selective responsibility.

The broader significance of revisiting Bandung within the context of a book on the history of the United Nations is to demonstrate that international relations are not simply about the relationship of the West to the rest of the world. Phạm and Shilliam put this succinctly by saying that 'these other international relations are not "other-worldly"; they operate in this world, but through non-conventional points of departures, thought systems, archives, sensibilities, aspirations and practices that variously contest, provincialize or re-entangle themselves with the global-colonial projection of power and order' (2016, 4). So, to place Bandung into the history of the United Nations is not to simply recognise two events happening simultaneously but to connect these two spaces to one another more intricately. It demonstrates the narrowness of international relations that tells the history of the United Nations only from the perspective of the West and the West's desire to 'help' the rest of the world to 'develop'.

Chapter 5

After Bandung

Independence and Non-alignment

Bandung was closely followed by decolonisation and political independence for large parts of the world, and yet, for reasons already established here, political and economic hierarchies of colonialism remained. This chapter explores the priorities and demands of groups that have sought to hold the permanent members of the Security Council to account from the 1960s onwards. Drawing upon archival material, this brief overview demonstrates the extent to which colonialism continues to impact the economic and political ordering of the world and some of the alternatives that have been proposed via the Non-Aligned Movement, UNCTAD, the G77 and the New Asian-African Strategic Partnership. The existence of these groups post-decolonisation – although varied in their membership, strategies and successes – signifies a continued mistrust of the major powers and resistance to the neocolonial forms of domination and exploitation facilitated by the United Nations and its structure. Within the context of this book, these discussions are important in terms of challenging the United Nations and the major powers' continued reliance on the concept of responsibility. The issues raised by these groups reinforce the impact of histories of colonisation and highlight the hypocrisy of the major powers who claim to be acting in the interests of international peace and security while perpetuating inequality.

THE UNITED NATIONS, DECOLONISATION AND INDEPENDENCE

In December 1960, the mounting pressure for decolonisation within the United Nations resulted in General Assembly Resolution 1514, also known as the Declaration on the Granting of Independence to Colonial Countries and Peoples. The proposal originally came from the Soviet Union, but the version adopted came from a collaboration of African and Asian member states, based largely on the Bandung principles and saw abstentions from European member states as well as the United States (Mazower 2012). The Declaration stated that:

1. The subjection of peoples to alien subjugation, domination and exploitation constitutes a denial of fundamental human rights, is contrary to the Charter of the United Nations and is an impediment to the promotion of world peace and cooperation.
2. All peoples have the right to self-determination; by virtue of that right they freely determine their political status and freely pursue their economic, social and cultural development.
3. Inadequacy of political, economic, social or educational preparedness should never serve as a pretext for delaying independence.
4. All armed action or repressive measures of all kinds directed against dependent peoples shall cease in order to enable them to exercise peacefully and freely their right to complete independence, and the integrity of their national territory shall be respected.
5. Immediate steps shall be taken, in Trust and Non-Self-Governing Territories or all other territories which have not yet attained independence, to transfer all powers to the peoples of those territories, without any conditions or reservations, in accordance with their freely expressed will and desire, without any distinction as to race, creed or colour, in order to enable them to enjoy complete independence and freedom.
6. Any attempt aimed at the partial or total disruption of the national unity and the territorial integrity of a country is incompatible with the purposes and principles of the Charter of the United Nations.
7. All States shall observe faithfully and strictly the provisions of the Charter of the United Nations, the Universal Declaration of Human Rights and the present Declaration on the basis of equality, non-interference in the internal affairs of all States, and respect for the sovereign rights of all peoples and their territorial integrity. (United Nations 1960)

In words not dissimilar to those used in the Final Communiqué of the Bandung Conference in 1955, this declaration signalled an acknowledgement of the contradictory rhetoric of the Charter. It asserts that colonisation amounts to a denial of human rights and that a lack of economic, political or social development by whatever standards should never serve as a justification for colonisation. It also provides a critique of those systems within the United Nations that sought to maintain colonial rule through 'transitional' periods, demanding that independence should be granted without conditions.

This declaration and its adoption were unsurprising, given that 1960 had seen sixteen new states granted independence and membership to the United Nations, meaning the Asia-Africa bloc had forty-six out of ninety-nine votes in the General Assembly (Mazower 2009, 185). The strength of anti-colonial unity within the General Assembly could, therefore, no longer be ignored, and undoubtedly, decolonisation was an achievement of the anti-colonial movement that had grown in strength since the end of the First World War and the Paris Peace Conference. However, it was also the case that the leading powers of the United Nations began to see that decolonisation would be key for the continued existence of an international institution that legitimised their considerable global influence. This new majority in the General Assembly was one that the major powers needed to keep on their side if they wanted the United Nations to continue to exist, and so the process of worldwide decolonisation was inevitable (MacQueen 2011). Despite the strong commitment to decolonisation laid out in the United Nations' declaration, decolonisation was not so easily achieved in its fullest terms. As Fanon states, 'colonialism and imperialism have not paid their score when they withdraw their flags and their police forces from our territories' (1967, 79). This chapter explores the different ways in which non-Western states have attempted to hold the United Nations to account in the complex post-independence political environment.

THE NON-ALIGNED MOVEMENT

Early Years

The First Conference of Heads of State or Government of Non-Aligned Countries occurred in Belgrade from 1 to 6 September 1961. The declaration of this conference reaffirms many of the core principles present in the documents from Bandung, most notably: a desire to 'eradicate colonialism in all its manifestations' and a commitment to 'a firm foundation of cooperation and brotherhood between nations' (Non-Aligned Movement 1961, 6–7). However, while non-alignment is featured in debates at Bandung, Vitalis (2013) recommends caution in seeing the Non-Aligned Movement as an *extension* of Bandung. Rather, non-alignment emerged as a rival to Bandung and those who pursued a second Bandung conference on the basis that the range of economic and political ideologies present at Bandung was too wide for agreement (Vitalis 2013). Nonetheless, the Non-Aligned Movement focused not just on independence but also justice for those formerly colonised, through equitable participation in the global economy. Although their name came from the strategy of taking no side in the Cold War, their

demands went beyond this in outlining economic strategies for newly independent states.

Meeting a year after the United Nations Declaration on the Granting
of Independence to Colonial Countries and Peoples, the Non-Aligned
Movement remained focused on the significant and detrimental consequences
of colonialism, particularly in economic terms. Justice for the colonised
would not be achieved solely through the granting of political independence,
and so the 1961 declaration argues that

> efforts should be made to remove economic imbalance inherited from
> colonialism and imperialism. They consider it necessary to close, through
> accelerated economic, industrial and agricultural development, the ever-
> widening gap in the standards of living between the few economically advanced
> countries and the many economically less-developed countries. (NAM 1961, 9)

This first declaration demonstrates a clear understanding that colonialism has
impacted the structure of the world on more than a political level, so while
freedom for the colonies from imperial control politically is essential, it does
little to resolve the unequal balance of power on a global scale with regards
to economic development. It fails to recognise that some countries are rich
because other countries are poor. A heavy focus of this first conference was,
therefore, to establish strategies for redressing the balance and ensuring fair
terms of trade, although a coherent ideological position in this sense was
difficult to establish (Prashad 2007).

In addressing the ongoing political context of the Cold War, the Belgrade
declaration states:

> The Governments of countries participating in the Conference resolutely reject
> the view that war, including the 'cold war', is inevitable, as this view reflects a
> sense both of helplessness and hopelessness and is contrary to the progress of
> the world. They affirm their unwavering faith that the international community
> is able to organize its life without resorting to means which actually belong to a
> past epoch of human history. (NAM 1961, 7)

It also reinforces a need for 'general, complete and strictly internationally
controlled disarmament'. Again, following the strong message of disarmament from Bandung, this first declaration of the Non-Aligned Movement
takes a clear anti-war position and emphasises the necessity of international
cooperation in preventing war globally. In addition to this, the declaration
reaffirms faith in the United Nations but only on the condition that the membership of both the Security Council and the Economic and Social Council is
increased to more adequately serve its expanded membership (NAM 1961,

10). While this collective exists externally to the United Nations, it was from the outset committed to reform within the United Nations rather than calling for its abolition. The range of political positions and economic conditions within countries that identified themselves as non-aligned meant that this was not intended as a formal organisation in competition with the United Nations but as a conference of non-aligned states to discuss the need for reform of the United Nations (Dinkel 2019). Its demands in relation to reform are largely centred around expanded membership of key decision-making bodies to reflect equitable geographical distribution as a means of addressing the unequal power dynamics that were built into the United Nations via the Charter. This early declaration provides a critique of the ways in which the United Nations is built upon colonial power structures that enable war, rather than preventing it. The non-aligned states saw the United Nations as a crucial international forum but sought to democratise it through expanding the role of the General Assembly (Prashad 2007).

The second conference of the Non-Aligned Movement was held in Cairo in 1964. The declaration of this conference starts out by acknowledging the success of the Non-Aligned Movement, while also stating that 'the forces of imperialism are still powerful and that they do not hesitate to resort to the use of force to defend their interests and maintain their privileges' (NAM 1964, 2). The declaration goes on to say that the continued use of force by imperial powers is a threat to global peace, particularly in instances of neocolonialism, apartheid and racial discrimination (NAM 1964, 3). Despite four years passing since the Declaration on the Granting of Independence to Colonial Countries and Peoples, the conference recognised that this had not been implemented everywhere and that colonialism in a variety of forms was still in existence. The agenda of the Non-Aligned Movement was 'discursively grounded in the unfulfilled postwar ideals of national equality, democracy, multilateralism, and postcolonial interdependence' (Grovogui 1996, 191). They drew attention to the contradictions of the rhetoric of the United Nations and its declarations of equality and democracy. The declaration again calls out the contradictions of the Charter of the United Nations, which holds self-determination as one of its primary principles while failing to act in cases of continued colonisation:

> The Conference denounces the attitude of those powers which oppose the exercise of the right of peoples to self-determination. It condemns the use of force, and all forms of intimidation, interference and intervention which are aimed at preventing the exercise of this right. (NAM 1964, 11)

However, the ongoing use of force against the colonised was not the only concern of this second conference. The declaration also shows a continued focus on trade and development as core issues for the formerly colonised, acknowledging the positive step taken in organising the United Nations Conference on Trade and Development (UNCTAD), while arguing that 'much ground still remains to be covered to eliminate existing inequalities in the relationships between industrialized and developing countries' (NAM 1964, 3).

In the 1970s, UNCTAD went on to develop the New International Economic Order (NIEO) proposals that sought to oppose free market capitalism on the basis that it intensified existing inequalities, instead suggesting that developing countries needed intervention in the market to ensure equitable participation, including the power to regulate multinational corporations and to nationalise industry (Taylor and Smith 2007). As reflected in the previous chapter, to oppose neocolonialism was to challenge the expansion of global capitalism, which could only expand the financial gaps created by centuries of colonial exploitation and extraction. Non-aligned states considered their independence at risk through economic independence upon the West (Dinkel 2019). If these newly independent states were to participate in the global economy, it required at the very least some intervention into existing systems to ensure a level playing field. While the NIEO proposals ultimately failed with the worldwide implementation of neoliberalism, the early years of UNCTAD provided a space within the United Nations for formerly colonised states to discuss economic disadvantages and suggest practicable solutions to address them. The proposals framed the United Nations as an international space where redistribution beyond foreign aid or charity was possible (Getachew 2019). They argued that as a consequence of colonialism, the global economy had been structured in such a way that the global south was a site of extraction, and this ought to be remedied. As Taylor and Smith (2007) have noted, while UNCTAD made some limited gains in its early years, the material dominance of the West made it difficult to implement any real structural change, so it became primarily a site of contestation.

In making a case for economic reforms, the 1964 declaration of the Non-Aligned Movement goes on to say that poverty and a lack of economic development are not only significant for those countries that are suffering but that 'the persistence of poverty poses a threat to world peace and prosperity' (NAM 1964, 29). Framing the issue of poverty in this way challenges the individualisation of responsibility for economic development that is characteristic of capitalism. As Rodney notes, it is through the racist understandings of white supremacy that a lack of industrial development is understood as inherent inferiority of Africa/Africans in particular, rather than attributing this to the 'organized viciousness' of the colonial system (2012 [1972], 219). Part of the power of colonialism is its ability to present inequality as the natural order of things, rather than a conscious project of extraction and underdevelopment, whereby European or Western economic advantage is seen as the consequence of innovation and entrepreneurship without acknowledging the violence that makes this possible. Instead of seeing poverty as a problem for each state to reckon with, the Non-Aligned Movement frames poverty as a problem for the international community to address, and so challenges the idea that unequal economic development is natural and the consequence of a lack of innovation.

The positive acknowledgement of UNCTAD is reflective of a broader attitude present in the 1964 declaration, which demonstrates a firm belief in the United Nations as an institution on the basis that it is able to be reformed. The priorities for reform within the United Nations are listed as: independence for those still colonised; expanding the membership to all states globally; equitable geographical representation and adapting the Charter to better reflect the current international environment (NAM 1964, 28). The focus was on eliminating colonialism and active reform of systems and networks to address the inequalities that colonialism had caused. While the Non-Aligned Movement met outside of the formal boundaries of the United Nations, it demonstrated a commitment to reform rather than a reluctance to engage or to see an international community organised solely by regional affiliations. Dinkel (2019) has argued that the Non-Aligned Movement represented an opportunity and desire on the part of newly decolonised states to assert their legitimacy as international actors. As such, there remained a strong desire to participate in global organisations and international relations more broadly, working alongside the West, while recognising the need for these organisations to change in order to reflect better a newly decolonised world.

This commitment to strengthening the United Nations continued into the third and fourth conferences of the Non-Aligned Movement, in Lusaka in 1970 and Algiers in 1973, while also proposing means for cultivating self-reliance and regional cooperation. Ten years after the Declaration on the Granting of Independence to Colonial Countries and Peoples, the statement of the third conference of the Non-Aligned Movement highlights the continued influence of colonialism in terms of direct control – particularly with reference to apartheid in South Africa – and in relation to structural inequality. The 1970 declaration states 'that the persistence of an inequitable world economic system inherited from the colonial past and continued through present neo-colonialism poses insurmountable difficulties in breaking the bondage of poverty and the shackles of economic dependence' (NAM 1970, 81). Much of this document focuses on the ways in which states can support each other in developing their economies through trade relationships, the sharing of information regarding technology, preferential import charges and encouraging tourism. So, while the Non-Aligned Movement recognised colonialism as the root cause of inequality globally, it also acknowledged that it was unlikely that colonisers would rectify this themselves. A decade of campaigning for changes to the global economic system to address inequality had been largely unsuccessful in terms of Western capitulation.

For Singham and Hune (1986), the main achievement of the Non-Aligned Movement in these early years was its recognition of hegemony in its many forms as the major problem in the international arena. The Non-Aligned Movement, despite the conflicting ideological positions and economic circumstances of its members, acted as a counter-hegemonic force that refused alignment with the major powers. The role of the major powers within the United Nations is central to the arguments of this book, particularly in the way that they have been able to make claims to a burden of responsibility in maintaining international peace and security, but to enact this responsibility selectively. In reaffirming a belief in the potential of the United Nations, the 1973 declaration notes

> disregard for United Nations decisions and the tendency of great Powers to monopolize the Organization's activities, to render it inactive or to divert it to their own private interests, contradict the universal nature of the Organization and reduce its standing and prestige. (NAM 1973, 18)

As previously observed, the Cold War years were especially fraught in terms of relationships between the major powers within the Security Council, resulting in significant periods of inaction as a consequence of unprecedented use of the veto, as well as major powers using the General Assembly as a space to garner support. The 1973 conference called upon these states to 'show wisdom and moral integrity in the exercise of their functions' (NAM 1973, 18). The Non-Aligned Movement sought to hold the major powers to account in terms of their rhetoric of responsibility, demonstrating that for this argument to hold, the major powers were required to exercise this responsibility fairly and consistently. To use the United Nations as an arena for their disagreements and the furthering of their political interests was to show the world that the United Nations' claims to universality were a pretence and reduced the legitimacy of the organisation as a whole.

In the eyes of the Non-Aligned Movement, if the United Nations retained any sense of global importance, it required the major powers to relinquish some level of control by expanding membership and acting in accordance with the principles enshrined in the Charter. These early years of the Non-Aligned Movement were focused on addressing the global economic imbalance caused by colonisation through the regulation of the market and serious reform of the United Nations, particularly in relation to the continued dominance of the major powers. The Non-Aligned Movement saw peace and security as inherently tied to eliminating poverty and equitable participation in the global economy for all states.

After the Cold War

The early years of the Non-Aligned Movement were unsurprisingly its most active and proactive in making demands for reform, although the movement continued through the 1970s and 1980s. The economic development of newly industrialised states during these two decades, however, had deepened some of the cracks between member states (Alden et al. 2010). The ninth conference of the Non-Aligned Movement met in Belgrade in September of 1989, just before the fall of the Berlin Wall and the declaration of the end of the Cold War. At this conference, the movement celebrated its success in the struggle against colonialism, neocolonialism and apartheid but maintained the same priorities in terms of disarmament, economic development and self-determination (NAM 1989). However, almost thirty years after the United Nations declared a commitment to independence for the colonies, this document noted that there were still countries living under imperial rule and that this was 'incompatible with the aspiration of freedom, sovereignty and peace of the peoples of the world and with the principles and purposes of the Movement of Non-Aligned Countries' (NAM 1989, 59). The United Nations had declared 1990–2000 as the 'Decade for the Elimination of Colonialism' and the time for the complete implementation of the commitment made in 1960. The 1989 declaration of the Non-Aligned Movement welcomed this but went further than previous declarations in arguing that colonial powers should also take on as their responsibility reparations for the economic, social and cultural consequences of colonisation (NAM 1989, 59). In this document, we see a shift from recognising of the consequences of colonisation and the need for an international commitment to addressing the subsequent inequalities to an explicit suggestion that colonising countries themselves should pay a debt to those they had exploited.

This shift from requesting support for economic development to a demand for reparations was partly fuelled by a worsening economic situation in the developing world. The advent of neoliberalism as a global economic system and the subsequent debt crisis in the global south had resulted in a greater wealth gap between the world's richest and poorest countries. As Prashad (2014) outlines in detail, neoliberalism saw the global powers seek to restore their position of dominance following the gains made by newly decolonised states. Following the failure of the NIEO proposals, these states turned to Western finance, which came with many strings attached. The 1989 declaration of the Non-Aligned Movement identifies this as an urgent issue that affects political stability and, therefore, the maintenance of international peace and security (NAM 1989).

Fifty Years of Non-alignment

The year 2011 marked fifty years since the formal establishment of the Non-Aligned Movement. This anniversary fell shortly after the global financial crash of 2007–2008 and at a time when the Security Council was under increased scrutiny regarding instances of military intervention. The lengthy statement from the 2011 Ministerial Conference and Commemorative Meeting of the Non-Aligned Movement in Bali reflects on this and demonstrates a continued commitment to the prevention of war and the extinction of colonialism in all its forms. This statement notes that the United Nations declared 2011–2020 as the 'Third International Decade for the Eradication of Colonialism' and urged the international community to increase the speed with which this would be achieved while also reaffirming a belief in the necessity of reparative or compensatory payments from colonising states for the consequences of their occupations (NAM 2011, 24). This statement provides a wealth of suggestions for reform of the United Nations in order to enable the organisation to work for the best interests of all states and avoid the domination of the major powers.

To this end, the 2011 statement requests an overhaul of the Security Council, including 'the question of membership, regional representation, the Council's agenda, its working methods and decision-making process, including the veto' (NAM 2011, 36). These are questions raised at San Francisco in 1945 and have become increasingly pertinent in the last two decades. As the 2011 conference notes, 'the Security Council has been too quick to threaten or authorise enforcement action in some cases while being silent and inactive in others' (NAM 2011, 36). This document thus provides a critique of the selectivity of the Security Council and its growing influence in other areas of the United Nations' work, such as economic development. It notes the increasingly interventionist approach that has been taken by states since the end of the Cold War, despite agreement on the Responsibility to Protect principle in 2001, which sought to clarify appropriate instances for intervention as a last resort. In order to address this, the Non-Aligned Movement made suggestions for the enlargement of the Council, including enhanced representation of Africa as an acknowledgement for its historical lack of representation (NAM 2011, 38). As will become more significant for the arguments developed in the next chapter, the conference states that they 'reject any attempts to use the Security Council to pursue national political agendas and stressed the necessity of non-selectivity and impartiality in the work of the Council' (NAM 2011, 38).

While cooperation between states in the global south is seen as essential for the maintenance of national and regional culture and mutual benefit, the economic development of these states must also be aided by states in the global north as a means of redistributing wealth. Over the course of its existence from 1961 to the present day, the Non-Aligned Movement has remained focused on addressing the material consequences of a history of colonisation, as well as seeking to reform the United Nations in order that it might act as an organisation fit to preserve peace and security for all nations. From 1961 to 2016, we see a continued commitment to improving the political, economic and social situation of formerly colonised states, with the Non-Aligned Movement calling upon the United Nations to implement fairly and consistently the principles enshrined in the Charter.

THE GROUP OF 77

The Group of 77 (G77) emerged to focus more specifically on the economic issues faced by developing countries within the United Nations. As previously noted, the United Nations Conference on Trade and Development (UNCTAD) was established in 1964, following concerns raised at Bandung and by the Non-Aligned Movement about the inequalities of international trade and the impact on developing countries. Since this first conference, it has become a permanent body within the United Nations, meeting every four years (UNCTAD 2022). At the end of the first UNCTAD conference, the seventy-seven developing countries in attendance issued a joint declaration and since then have existed as an alliance, although their membership now numbers 134. This initial declaration ends with the following statement:

> The United Nations Conference on Trade and Development marks the beginning of a new era in the evolution of international co-operation in the field of trade and development. Such co-operation must serve as a decisive instrument for ending the division of the world into areas of affluence and intolerable poverty. This task is the outstanding challenge of our times. The injustice and neglect of centuries need to be redressed. The developing countries are united in their resolve to continue to quest for such redress and look to the entire international community for understanding and support in this endeavour. (Group of 77 1964, 2)

This primary declaration recognises that UNCTAD is a positive step in holding the international community to account in relation to trade and development for the formerly colonised. It reflects the feeling that eliminating global poverty is the responsibility of all states within the United Nations and that a redistribution of wealth is required to address centuries of inequality and impoverishment. The G77 states also recognised that their unity was required in order to attempt to balance the weight of the Organisation for Economic Co-Operation and Development (Toye 2014).

Following three decades of pressure from the G77, secretary general of the United Nations Kofi Annan presented a report to the General Assembly in 1997 entitled *Renewing the United Nations: A Programme for Reform*, which sought to 'identify the ways in which the United Nations can more effectively and efficiently meet the challenges that lie ahead as we enter a new century and a new millennium' (United Nations 1997, 2). The report put forward proposals for changes to the structure of the United Nations, primarily through streamlining the Secretariat, as well as identifying 'sustained and sustainable development' as a central priority (United Nations 1997). It celebrated the successes of the United Nations – proudly claiming decolonisation as one of its greatest achievements – while also acknowledging that 'neither governments, nor the United Nations, nor the private sector has found the key to eradicating the persistent poverty that grips the majority of humankind. Indeed, imbalances in the world economy today pose serious challenges to future international stability' (United Nations 1997, 9). For the G77, *Renewing the United Nations* was a welcome assessment of the need for the United Nations to do more to address global inequality but did not go far enough in addressing the concerns of developing countries.

To this end, they provided a lengthy response to the report, which reiterated concerns around the prioritisation of global north interests within the United Nations. In their identification of the challenges faced by the United Nations going into the new millennium, the G77 asked:

a. Is the United Nations to be excluded for all practical purposes from having a significant voice and role in matters which are critical for the present and the future of humanity, in particular for the countries and peoples of the South? And is it to be increasingly transformed into an instrument virtually controlled by the most powerful nations to promote their geopolitical and economic interests, and the corresponding global regimes and disciplines?, or

b. Is the UN to be properly mandated, financed and equipped to pursue as a democratic, pluralistic organization, the multiple complex tasks enshrined in its Charter, working to offset the mounting unilateralism inherent in the current highly asymmetrical world order? And should the organization contribute creatively to defining, shaping, and managing a world order which both resolves longstanding problems and meets the new challenges faced by the international community?' (Group of 77 1997, 2)

For the G77, the United Nations' report amounted to an acceptance of the status quo and the existing global economic order, refocusing the organisation's attention to issues of peace and security and allowing economic concerns to be dealt with by the IMF and the WTO. Their response states that 'while such a policy may be an attempt to accommodate the current realities of economic and political power, it is clearly contrary to the UN Charter and the very purpose and inspiration of the organization' (Group of 77 1997, 3).

On the issue of peace and security, the G77 expressed discontent with the suggestion that peacekeeping be the domain of those states with 'capabilities' given that this is likely to limit the number of states involved in those kinds of decisions. They argued that one of the primary challenges for the United Nations was and is 'how to make peacekeeping more democratic and participatory and to prevent it from becoming a tool for the unilateral pursuit of policies by a few powerful countries', linking this to a necessary reform of the Security Council (Group of 77 1997, 10). For the G77, this report represented the United Nations resigning itself to only working within the realms of the feasible given existing political and economic structures and relegating 'the notion of democracy in international relations to the realm of a utopian illusion' (Group of 77 1997, 15). Despite its flaws, the United Nations still seemed to represent the only arena for developing countries to exercise influence over global affairs, and yet the 1997 report amounted to an acceptance of the existing global order rather than a continued fight towards equality.

BANDUNG AND THE NEW ASIAN-AFRICAN STRATEGIC PARTNERSHIP

In addition to the continued work of the Non-Aligned Movement and the G77, the 1955 conference at Bandung was celebrated on its fiftieth anniversary, with leaders of African and Asian states meeting in Jakarta to 'reinvigorate the spirit of Bandung' and work towards the development of a New Asian-African Strategic Partnership (NAASP) (Asian-African Summit 2005, 1). This partnership was designed to ensure continued cooperation between African and Asian states based on mutual respect in spite of differences, and the declaration issued during this conference reiterated the core principles of Bandung as solidarity, friendship and cooperation in the interests of resolving global issues (Asian-African Summit 2005, 1). This partnership was, however, imagined differently in the sense of existing outside of government relationships and seeing a greater role for industry and business as a consequence of Asia's growing economic status (Alden et al. 2010). The 2005 declaration reaffirmed a commitment established at

Bandung for African and Asian states to work together for mutual benefit in a range of arenas, including trade, industry, finance, energy, health and transport.

In line with the ideas of the majority of what has been considered here as transnational anti-colonial solidarity movements since 1955, the 2005 declaration states a commitment to demanding reform of the United Nations rather than a rejection of this platform. The NAASP's 'Plan of Action' states that political cooperation between states in the global south will include:

Promoting the reform of the United Nations with the aims of strengthening multilateralism, reinforcing the role of the United Nations in maintaining and promoting international peace, security and sustainable development, as well as ensuring greater participation for and share among Asian and African countries in its decision-making processes. (Asian-African Summit 2005, 8)

As with the Non-Aligned Movement and the G77, the NAASP recognised that the United Nations was still the best option available to African and Asian states in terms of an international organisation, despite its flaws. Rather than seeking to develop an alternative South-South organisation, the NAASP remained committed to pushing for greater participation within this existing framework.

This commitment to United Nations reform is also stated in the 2015 declaration at the sixtieth-anniversary summit, albeit with more specific aims:

Reiterating the principle and benefits of multilateralism, we resolve to further strengthen and support the United Nations and other multilateral and regional forums so they work more effectively towards strengthening peace and prosperity in Asia and Africa as well as other regions. We call for continued efforts to reform the United Nations, including the revitalization of the General Assembly and a comprehensive reform of the Security Council, which corresponds to the collective interests of developing countries. A reformed Security Council will significantly increase representation of Asia and Africa. (Asian-African Summit 2015, 1)

The ten years between the fiftieth- and sixtieth-anniversary celebrations had seen increasing scrutiny of the Security Council, particularly regarding its interventions in the Middle East and North Africa, which provides important political context for this summit. As a result, the declaration in 2015 argues specifically for increased representation on the Security Council along with comprehensive reform, as well as improving the role of the General Assembly as a decision-making body within the United Nations, all of which amount to a more direct challenge to the continued dominance of the major powers within the organisation. However, if this declaration left any doubt about the mood of the sixtieth-anniversary summit, the opening speech is more explicit.

In opening the Asian-African Summit of 2015, the president of Indonesia, Joko Widodo, made a stronger statement on global inequality, linking it directly to a history of colonialism. Widodo reminded delegates that despite the achievements made in the sixty years since the first Asian-African Conference, 'our struggle is far from over' (Widodo 2015, 1). While the first conference in 1955 saw several representatives present who were still under direct colonial rule, 2015 saw these representatives come together on behalf of independent states. However, this did not mean that the aims of the 1955 conference had been fully realised or that justice for those colonies had been achieved. For Widodo, global injustice centres around the unequal distribution and consumption of resources: 'When the rich nations, which comprise a mere 20 percent of the world's population, consume 70 percent of the world resources, then global injustice becomes real' (Widodo 2015, 1). Thus, justice would require a redistribution of resources and holding to account those nations that disproportionately consume them. Addressing the distribution of wealth and resources would also require reform of international financial institutions in light of emerging economic powers (Widodo 2015). Widodo's speech is important in two respects: firstly, it reinforces the idea that colonialism does not end with independence but with justice and redistribution; and secondly, that the world has changed and our institutions must change with it, acknowledging that the power afforded to Europe and the United States is disproportionate to their economic weight in the twenty-first century.

Widodo's speech is also more forceful in its condemnation of interventionist policy and military action by major powers within the United Nations framework. Where other declarations have reiterated the need to respect sovereignty and self-determination, Widodo explicitly addressed the use of force by major powers and its impact on the United Nations' capacity to maintain international peace and security:

When a group of rich countries think that they could change the world by the use of force, the global inequality clearly brings about misery, of which the United Nations looks helpless. The use of unilateral force without a clear UN mandate, as we have witnessed, has undermined the existence of our common world body. Therefore, we, the nations of Asia and Africa, demands the UN reform, so that it could function better, as a world body that puts justice for all of us before anything else. (Widodo 2015, 2)

This commentary addresses a range of issues surrounding the capacity of the United Nations to protect international peace and security and to challenge military might in its current format. Widodo's request for reform of the United Nations on this basis brings us full circle to the reservations seen at San Francisco in 1945 about the structure of the Security Council and the privilege afforded to the major powers, demonstrating how little has changed.

AFTER BANDUNG

This chapter has provided an overview of some of the key anti-colonial movements since 1955 to sketch out the priorities and demands that have been made of the United Nations, as well as highlighting some of the internal contradictions of these movements. There are and were, of course, a whole host of other transnational movements working towards justice for the colonised and economic/political partnerships outside of Western capitalism – too many to cover here. These movements can be understood collectively as the Third World, which acted as a moral space to consider issues that fell outside of the realms of the West's interests, enabling cooperation between postcolonial states (Grovogui 2016). While this chapter has shown a deep engagement with issues within the context of the United Nations, these movements are often viewed as separate from international politics during this period, as not within the realm of 'proper' international politics. These archival documents show that the Third World provided a contestation of the existing global order and alternative visions.

The summary provided here has established that decolonisation in the form of the United Nations Declaration on the Granting of Independence to Colonial Countries and Peoples did not signal the end of colonial power dynamics and structures. As the earlier chapters of this book have demonstrated, these power dynamics were built into the very structures of the organisation such that political decolonisation could happen without unsettling the existing global order. This is not to say that there have been no changes since 1960, but that these changes have done little to change the fate of the world's poorest nations which were most affected by the extractive exploitation of colonialism, and these changes have done little to address the power retained by former imperial states within global organisations. The United Nations in 2022 looks very similar to the United Nations of 1945.

While the Non-Aligned Movement, the G77 and the Asia-Africa Summit have worked across different institutional spaces from 1955 to now, documents from their archives identify two primary and related concerns: economic inequality and institutional reform. The Declaration on the Granting of Independence to Colonial Countries and Peoples in 1960 coincided with a particular political moment where it seemed that imperial powers were losing their grip, but the work of these anti-colonial movements since then demonstrates the extent to which colonial power dynamics are built into the structure of the United Nations and the global economic system. Revisiting these movements and the demands that they have made historically is important in providing a continued challenge to the United Nations' claims to equality, universality and a commitment to finding shared solutions to common problems, as well as challenging a continued reliance on the idea of responsibility. The refusal to reform the United Nations demonstrates the ways in which the narrative of 'development' enables the preservation of the existing global order by always privileging the rights of the world's most powerful who are able to operate through selective responsibility. The archival documents examined here remind us that an alternative vision exists and that the United Nations does not stand unchallenged.

Chapter 6

From Non-intervention to R2P

The purpose of this final chapter is to make the connection between contemporary debates surrounding the United Nations and its history that has been the focus of this book thus far. The Charter of the United Nations outlines a commitment to non-intervention in the domestic affairs of other states, which stands in contrast to the current policy of Responsibility to Protect, which amounts to states having a *responsibility* to intervene in the domestic affairs of other states. This chapter charts the shift from the principle of non-intervention to the policy of Responsibility to Protect, making the argument that Responsibility to Protect is a neocolonial technology that draws upon colonial discourses, framing particular nations as uncivilised and in need of education by wiser, more civilised nations. While the principle of Responsibility to Protect has had significant attention within international relations literature, here we read these contemporary debates through the historical events discussed so far and put these contemporary issues into conversation with the past that enables them to emerge. It is here, then, that the concept of *selective responsibility* applies most clearly.

The sixty years between the signing of the Charter of the United Nations and the agreement on the principle of Responsibility to Protect at the World Summit of 2005 has seen distinct periods of development in terms of approaches to intervention, which will be examined in some detail here. Beginning with the significance of non-intervention after the Second World War, then moving on to look at how the United Nations was affected by disputes between the superpowers during the Cold War, followed by an examination of the rise of humanitarian intervention, particularly during the 1990s and the ICISS report on Responsibility to Protect that followed in 2001, we can see the development of the idea of responsibility as central to United Nations policy. While this development of this policy is often framed in terms of a humanitarian response to atrocities, policies within the United Nations and their application to real-life scenarios are always heavily influenced by issues of global political power, and, in this particular instance, the notion of 'responsibility' is often used to conceal particular political interests and strategies. This chapter brings together the argument running throughout the book that the process of decolonisation and the eventual disbanding of the trusteeship system in 1994 resulted in the need for new forms of control and domination and that this was done under the guise of responsibility that sprung from discourses of development and civilisation that were established through colonisation. While states and their representatives may also feel genuine concern for the suffering of individuals, the concept of selective responsibility within this context functions as a neocolonial technology of power to ensure the continuation of ideas around civilisation and development that maintain the existing – unequal – global order. The major powers make political decisions about if and when to act upon their responsibilities.

This chapter presents an application of the theoretical perspective developed throughout the book to contemporary debates surrounding military intervention and humanitarianism to exemplify the relevance of an accurate understanding of the United Nations' history. It provides a timely example of the significance of understanding the history of the United Nations if we are to understand the ways in which it functions today. This chapter signifies the culmination of the arguments of the book and demonstrates the manifestations of postcolonial privilege and discourses of development and progress in the recent selective enforcement of policy relating to intervention.

NON-INTERVENTION AFTER THE
SECOND WORLD WAR

To reiterate, the preamble of the Charter of the United Nations states that in signing the Charter, member states agreed 'to unite our strength to maintain international peace and security, and to ensure, by the acceptance of principles and the institution of methods, that armed force shall not be used, save in the common interest' (United Nations 1945, 2). The Charter, signed following the end of the Second World War, was, therefore, designed to deal with wars between states rather than wars within states; it was designed to deal with international rather than domestic conflicts (Doyle and Sambanis 2006). With the sovereignty of states as a fundamental principle, the United Nations was designed to mediate relationships between individual states to maintain international peace and security, not to deal with internal conflicts within a sovereign state. Following on from its predecessor, the League of Nations, the wording of the preamble strongly infers that the United Nations was designed as a grouping of independent states in agreement to reduce the use of military force to prevent conflict on the scale of the First and Second World Wars. Indeed, as previously quoted, Article 2 of the Charter deals with the use of force by member states and dictates that, with regard to intervention:

> Nothing contained in the present Charter shall authorize the United Nations to intervene in matters which are essentially within the domestic jurisdiction of any state or shall require the Members to submit such matters to settlement under the present Charter. (United Nations 1945)

The Charter sets out the aims of the United Nations not as a world government but as an organisation designed to encourage international cooperation without interference in domestic matters.

The United Nations was, in this sense, intended as a Westphalian system of peacekeeping, whereby independent sovereign states were obliged to obey a particular set of rules of behaviour with regards to international relations, and as such the conflict would, in theory, only arise when states disobeyed the rules and acted aggressively towards each other (MacQueen 2011). Conflicts within states were not initially imagined to be within the realms of United Nations peacekeeping, and the right of those states recognised as sovereigns to manage their own domestic affairs was of the utmost importance. Although the United Nations' claims to universality and equality have already been questioned in terms of the very structure of the organisation, it aimed to *present* itself as universalist where the League of Nations had been criticised for being imperialist, and the principle of non-intervention was fundamental in its ability to do so. The principle of non-intervention in this context was not based on justice or moral grounds but on maintaining order, providing clear rules for limiting the use of force and reducing the risk of military conflict (Roberts 1993). For this new international organisation to function efficiently, it was considered necessary to provide clear guidelines on respecting the sovereignty of individual states and their ability to govern without the risk of intervention.

The United Nations Security Council has historically been respectful of this foundational principle of non-intervention and has privileged this over the right of individuals not to be killed (Bellamy 2011). Although the authenticity of this claim has been questioned in the earlier chapters of this book, the United Nations was in theory based on the sovereign equality of all its members, and as such non-intervention was the logical principle for governing relations between states or as Weiss puts it, 'the other side of the Westphalian coin' (2012, 21). If the United Nations was based on the equal right of all member states to maintain sovereign authority over their territory, this right had to be supported by the inability of any state to intervene in the affairs of another. This principle of non-intervention was of particular significance for those states joining the United Nations that had previously been the colonies of empire. At a time when the anti-colonial movement was gaining momentum and public attitudes had shifted in support of decolonisation, it was important to ensure that this new organisation would not support previous structures of domination. Indeed, the commitment to non-intervention and non-interference as outlined by the United Nations both in San Francisco and the Charter was the reason for so many states agreeing to join in the first instance (Roberts 1993). An organisation that committed to the independence and sovereignty of each of its members seemed an attractive prospect to those states that had suffered decades of exploitation and domination. For smaller, developing states, their commitment to membership in the United Nations was dependent upon a commitment by the world's most powerful states to respect their sovereignty and their right to rule within their own national borders (Mazower 2009). As the archives show, the sacrifice of sovereignty made by those smaller powers in the signing of the Charter and agreeing to the dominance of the five permanent members of the Security Council was frequently articulated, with representatives of those smaller powers stating that this was done on the understanding that the Security Council would guarantee collective security and the repression of acts of aggression (United Nations General Assembly 1946). Those states that had fought for independence were wary from the outset that while the promise of sovereign equality and formal independence was appealing, the United Nations had the capacity to become an arena for justifying postcolonial rule.

In later years, the principle of non-intervention continued to have a strong significance in debates around changing policies on intervention and approaches to dealing with humanitarian emergencies quickly and effectively. A number of largely ex-colonial states argued against developing norms of interventionist policy and maintained a fundamental commitment to non-intervention in the domestic affairs of other states as a governing approach (Mayall 1991). For formerly colonised states, the United Nations provided the opportunity to be treated as equal sovereigns with colonisers, and the principle of non-intervention formed the foundation for this relationship. While still colonised, these countries used the United Nations to fight against empire and to push for decolonisation, but once independent, these countries fought to keep the United Nations out of affairs that they understood to fall under their own domestic jurisdiction. This mood was indicative of an increasing concern around the inequality of power between states in the global system, particularly once the United Nations had proved itself to be a space for the privileging major power interests. However, as many of the governments of ex-colonial states fighting for non-intervention were dictatorships, their public commitment to liberalism as the basis for non-intervention failed to convince the international community, and as a result the increasingly interventionist approach of the major powers was not thwarted (Mayall 1991). Thus, while the Charter of the United Nations, on the surface, proclaimed non-intervention as an essential component of the organisation, the reality has increasingly distanced itself from this rhetoric. The concept of responsibility that was central to colonial discourses continued through the early years of the United Nations, justifying the position of the major powers while enabling them to enact this responsibility selectively.

POWER POLITICS IN THE COLD WAR PERIOD

The Cold War period saw a move away from this initial commitment to non-intervention, although without moving as strongly towards the humanitarian approach of the 1990s. International intervention by the United Nations during the Cold War period was based on a triumvirate of consent, neutrality and the use of force only in self-defence (MacQueen 2011). Intervention was to be authorised by the state in question, based on the restoration of peace rather than supporting a particular party in the case of a civil conflict, and intervening parties were not to use military action except where it was absolutely necessary to protect troops. This approach signified a move away from traditional forms of international peacekeeping and the principle of non-interference in domestic affairs as outlined in the Charter, but intervention remained heavily restricted and dependent upon the consent of states understood to be in need of international support. The Carter administration in the United States (from 1977 to 1981) was particularly keen to avoid military interference, highlighting the responsibility of the United States to act in accordance with international law (Cohen 2012). The United Nations, although perhaps only on the surface, remained reluctant to respond militarily to domestic disputes without the approval of the state concerned.

As the Cold War rumbled on, concerns were raised about the role of the major powers in implementing policies on intervention, with the structure of the Security Council coming into question. At a time when a number of bodies within the United Nations were subject to reform, the Security Council was paralysed in terms of efficiency due to the conflict between East and West (Bertrand 1995). The exclusivity of the Security Council and the crucial power of veto held by the five permanent members meant that it was impossible to secure an agreement on international security matters. Both the United States and the Soviet Union used their veto power frequently during this period to prevent action that would benefit the political interests of their enemy. As chapter 3 showed, this was exactly the concern of some of the smaller states present at the founding of the United Nations, who were assured that the activities of the Security Council were governed by the Charter and that the right to veto was a reflection of the burden of responsibility upon the five permanent members. The Cold War period confirmed that these concerns were not unfounded, with the major powers practising selective responsibility based on their own political interests. In addition, outside of the Security Council, the General Assembly also lost the sense of democracy and neutrality that was so important to the smaller member states. Instead, it became a showground for conflict between the superpowers who fought to generate allegiance from smaller states on matters of conflict upon finding the Security Council an ineffective route to action (Sayward 2013). The General Assembly had quickly become the only space within which the superpowers were able to propose action and gain support from those smaller member states that were not involved in the politics of the Security Council, but this was at the expense of other 'smaller' concerns. Global political relationships between states had a heavy impact on voting patterns and consequently upon the United Nations' capacity to take action as a supposedly neutral international institution.

Inside the General Assembly, the key focus of the United Nations' work during this period was promoting the idea of development for newly independent states, and the superpowers used this as an opportunity both to gain support and further their own policy agendas (Sayward 2013). Both Soviet and American forces emphasised their desire to work on projects that would promote and stimulate development for those states that had recently gained independence. However, the United States was evidently more convincing in its approach as it acquired huge levels of support from former colonies within the General Assembly, which was enough to ensure that almost all decisions made within the General Assembly privileged the US interests (Rowe 1971). In exchange for their commitment to promoting development, the United States received significantly increased support in relation to other issues presented in the General Assembly. This was particularly important in light of the Security Council's inability to act as a result of the constant invocation of the veto. This period clearly demonstrated the possibility of manipulating the United Nations as an institution in line with the political agendas of the most powerful nations, with decision-making reliant on the political relationships between states.

As outlined in earlier chapters, this idea of development as promoted by the United Nations is one that has formed the basis of international relationships since the colonial era. This discourse of development for former colonial territories that were crucial for the major powers throughout the Cold War period is grounded in a Western notion of progress and encourages a hierarchical relationship of dependence, with 'advanced' Western nations acting as teachers, guiding the uncivilised along a linear path to civilisation (Patil 2008). Rather than encouraging independence and respect for difference, the notion of development within this context assumes a singular goal for all states: Western liberalism. The independence of former colonies then becomes bound up in these problematic ideologies of development and civilisation that further legitimate the institutionalisation of great power privilege within the United Nations. This discourse justifies the position of the major powers and naturalises a hierarchy established by the unnatural colonial relationship, reinforcing the capacity for selective responsibility. The major powers defended their position within the organisation through the language of responsibility and paternalism, while as we saw in the previous chapter, refusing to make any significant strides towards reform that would facilitate economic or political development for the former colonies (Taylor and Smith 2007). During the Cold War period, the United States, in particular, used this problematic framing of global relationships to its benefit to gain support in its battle against communism.

The Security Council was not quite so easily manipulated in support of the United States' interests as the General Assembly. While the Soviet Union clearly used its power of veto as a political tool within the Security Council throughout the Cold War, it had also become particularly sceptical about the idea of military intervention, viewing it as an instrument of Western domination and interest (MacQueen 2011). Although the Security Council had historically respected the principle of non-interference, moves towards more interventionist policy raised concerns around the political agendas of the globally powerful. During the East-West conflict, the Security Council was prevented from taking action in the form of intervention on 212 occasions, largely at the hands of the Soviet Union (Weiss 2012). While this was undoubtedly in large part a political strategy and one element of a bigger battle between East and West, it was also representative of an increasing distrust of Western ideology and signified a protest against the continuing dominance of British and American forces in international politics.

The Cold War period, therefore, began to reveal the intricate networks of political power within the United Nations and how action and effectiveness could be manipulated at the hands of those governments at the top as a result of the strategic construction of the institution from its beginnings. While moves towards interventionist policy and the departure from non-intervention as a guiding principle were still in their infancy, what this period in the Security Council's history illustrates is that its permanent five members were able to use their position in order to ensure their political interests were being pursued, or at least to prevent action that was not in their interests. At San Francisco, these major powers had encouraged support for their permanent membership on the basis that they would be faced with the ultimate responsibility to act in the global interests, but the Cold War period illustrated the extent to which their own political interests would always be prioritised first and foremost – they operated a policy of selective responsibility. The increased emphasis on the discourse of development during this period is also significant for the changes in policy that followed and for understanding the ways in which power relationships established through colonialism were justified based on natural progression.

HUMAN RIGHTS AND HUMANITARIANISM IN THE 1990s

The 1990s and the end of the Cold War saw a further transformation in approaches to intervention. Encouraged by the relatively peaceful end to the conflict, the United Nations rearticulated a commitment to the foundational values of equality, freedom and liberalism (Barnett 2002). The dissolution of the Soviet Union had prompted within the United Nations a greater level of cooperation on security matters. While China remained vocal about its discomfort around the issue of intervention, this was not enough for it to invoke the power of veto (Higgins 1995). Where the Cold War had created political conflicts between East and West that had played out within the Security Council, the 1990s saw a much greater level of agreement on international security issues and a joint commitment to dealing with human rights abuses from an international perspective. There was, however, a sense in which existing policies and the focus on non-interference were not seen to be effective in dealing with the ever-rising number of humanitarian crises. As a result, the early 1990s saw an increasingly invasive interpretation of Chapter VII of the United Nations Charter (Doyle and Sambanis 2006).

This section of the Charter deals with 'Action with respect to threats to the peace, breaches of the peace, and acts of aggression' and details provisions for the Security Council to authorise the use of armed force in order to 'maintain or restore international peace and security' (United Nations 1945, 9). While previously, the United Nations had prioritised the right of sovereign states to rule without interference from the international community unless conflicts between states arose, a new form of intervention developed during this period, prioritising the rights of individuals to be treated in accordance with the United Nations Declaration of Human Rights (1948) over the right of states to non-intervention. Humanitarian concerns were not seen as a legitimate basis for military intervention during the Cold War period, but the 1990s saw a change in attitudes and the overwhelming acceptance of the idea that UN-authorised intervention was an appropriate response (Wheeler 2002). Humanitarianism became the norm for governing relations between states, and indeed between 1990 and 1999 the United Nations was responsible for leading thirty-five peace-keeping operations compared to only eighteen operations between 1948 and 1989 (United Nations 2016). This period, therefore, saw much greater emphasis being placed on the view that the international community has a duty to intervene, prevent and respond to instances of human rights abuse (Kaldor 2003). Where previously the United Nations had been framed as an organisation with the purpose of preventing international conflict, from the 1990s onwards, it began to take on a more active role in responding to the suffering of individuals within domestic contexts. It is helpful to briefly unpick the theoretical foundations that allowed humanitarianism to flourish to understand this shift.

The humanitarianism of the 1990s saw a greater level of importance accorded to the United Nations Declaration of Human Rights (1948) as a standard for the treatment of citizens by governments, alongside an increased emphasis on the obligation of the international community to ensure that all individuals were treated in accordance with it. Human rights as they are conceptualised by the United Nations within this declaration are grounded in a belief in common humanity and the idea that there is in all human beings the same basic moral conviction and, as such, a sense of solidarity. This conception of a common humanity asserts that we have a responsibility to assist anyone who is in need on the simple basis that they are our fellow human beings. The idea of humanity is, therefore, based on the understanding that all individuals, regardless of geographical location, are equal human beings with equal rights. Van Hooft (2011) explains this through the two separate but connected terms: 'Principle of Humanity' and 'Principle of Justice'. For Van Hooft (2011), the 'Principle of Humanity' leads to the 'Principle of Justice', which amounts to a duty to act to remedy issues of inequality. If you believe that we are all fundamentally equal human beings, then it follows that we have a responsibility to act when some are not being treated as such. The notion of justice here represents an acceptance that while all individuals have the right to be treated by the same universal standards, such as those outlined in the United Nations Declaration, this does not always happen and that through historical circumstances, inequalities exist between individuals and groups of individuals. Where inequality docs exist, the notion of humanity compels those who have the capacity to do so to address and attempt to deal with inequality, acting upon the notion of justice. The commonality underlying this idea of humanity and the commitment to justice is that of a shared vulnerability, which underpins human rights as a concept (Turner 2006). The humanitarianism of the 1990s is based on this understanding of a universal commitment to equality, justice and the equal treatment of all, as we are all equally vulnerable to abuse by our very existence as human beings.

Human rights as an ideology are built upon this foundation of common humanity that is not geographically located or temporally specific and which is held in the idea that we are all vulnerable to abuse of these rights at any given time. This sense of shared vulnerability and common humanity allows human rights (as policy) to be viewed as universally applicable and available to all through their status as human beings (Turner 2006). Thus, the moral foundation of human rights as a concept is discursively powerful, allowing human rights to be viewed as grounded in a basic human instinct to act in solidarity with others. This moral character provides human rights as a set of beliefs with a tone of rationality, constructing them as natural, neutral and outside the realm of politics (Douzinas 2007). This is problematic within the context of the United Nations as it has frequently allowed the major powers to justify intervention on the basis of these individual rights that are conceived of as natural and rational. However, this moral tone that frequently underpins discourses of human rights and underlies appeals to the use of intervention to protect human rights fails to acknowledge the historical construction of human rights as a concept. When we delve further into the history of human rights as an ideology, it becomes clear that they form part of the broader understanding of Western liberalism as the height of civilisation and the end point for human development.

The 1789 Rights of Man and Citizen are often cited as the predecessor of the United Nations Declaration of Human Rights and as the first attempt to formalise the rights of individuals. The Rights of Man, however, were never intended as universal rights for all individuals on the basis of their existence as human beings and were, in fact, a particular set of rights that were *not* applicable to certain groups, including women, enslaved people and criminals (Waters 1996). It is problematic, therefore, to view human rights as objectively universal when their historical origins are grounded in a set of rights that were deliberately exclusionary. The later inclusion of excluded groups fails to address how it is that the rights of a few became the rights of all and fails to address the historical processes that allowed for these initial silences (Bhambra and Shilliam 2009). To elaborate, the relationship between the United Nations Declaration of Human Rights and the exclusionary Rights of Man highlights the problematic historical basis of contemporary ideologies of human rights. Therefore, the use of the United Nations Declaration of Human Rights as a justification for interventions is also problematic in terms of the historic silencing of particular groups of individuals and particular cultures. While interventions based on the protection of human rights make claims to universality, the historical foundations of human rights as a concept are built upon privilege and so their use reinforces this privilege.

Nonetheless, human rights continue to be understood as a universal standard for the treatment of individuals, and they form the basis of the ideology of humanitarianism and subsequently the practice of humanitarian military intervention. The move towards humanitarianism after the Cold War and the subsequent development of humanitarian military intervention as legitimate action by the international community appeals to a sense of common humanity and a globalised duty to protect the rights of individuals or to seek justice where rights are being abused. Humanitarian military intervention in this sense is presented as a principle in line with the standard set at the Nuremberg trials after the Second World War, with the suggestion that if crimes against humanity can be used as the legal basis to prosecute individuals after events have taken place, then it can also be used as a basis for intervening to *prevent* humanitarian emergencies *before* they occur (Fine 2007). However, the concepts of common humanity and human rights have become synonymous with European/Western understandings of civilisation as a result of their historical development. This sense of common humanity underpinning the drive towards humanitarianism neglects the historical construction of human rights and contributes to the 'mystifying amnesia of the colonial aftermath' (Gandhi 1998, 4), whereby European culture is understood as universal culture without addressing the violence that accompanied the enforcement of this.

To refocus on the policy after this brief venture into the philosophy of rights, the development of humanitarian military intervention as a legitimate practice within the international community (and within the United Nations more specifically) was obviously not framed as a case of powerful nations intervening where they saw fit but as a practice that would increase the protection of individuals through an understanding of basic rights that are inherent in a civilised society and that are applicable to all human beings. However, it was the capacity of powerful nations to intervene where they saw fit that prompted scepticism and eventually led to a feeling of disillusionment with humanitarianism as a guiding principle for international relations (Blackburn 2010). In an attempt to address these concerns, cosmopolitan writers developed, and continue to support, a set of criteria that an international crisis must satisfy in order for humanitarian military intervention to be deemed legitimate. Wheeler (2002) argues that humanitarian intervention is only legitimate in cases where:

1. The situation can be deemed a 'supreme humanitarian emergency';
2. Force is used as a last resort;
3. A proportionality threshold is met, that is, the number of lives saved must outweigh the number of lives lost;
4. There is a high probability that the use of force will result in a positive humanitarian outcome.

For Wheeler (2002), all four of these requirements must be met for the intervention to be deemed legitimate. These criteria were developed to prevent situations whereby powerful nations manipulated the language of humanitarianism to justify interventions with ulterior motives. Although the conflict of the Cold War was no longer directly affecting decision-making within the United Nations, the concerns raised around the power politics of the institution remained at the forefront of approaches to intervention after 1989. Humanitarianism was heralded as a universal principle that would ensure that the United Nations was working on the basis of improving the lives of individuals without being led by selective responsibility and the political motivations of individual states.

Even if the criteria for legitimate intervention have been met, the conceptual danger of humanitarian military intervention lies in the construction of a victim/saviour dialectic, whereby developing nations play the role of the sufferer and powerful nations play the role of the rescuer (Douzinas 2007). The relationship between states within the framework of humanitarianism becomes a paternalistic relationship based on a responsibility to help those less fortunate, and although it is undeniable that the international community has some sort of duty to assist in cases of abuse, to allow international relationships to develop in this way is problematic as rescue is always based on a perceived superiority (Douzinas 2007). The policy of intervention based on humanitarianism, all too easily, becomes a legitimate form of cultural and political dominance through the language of development and responsibility, in much the same way as both the mandate system in the League of Nations and the trusteeship system in the early years of the United Nations. Powerful nations are able to justify their involvement in the political governance of developing nations under the guise of humanitarianism (Barnett 2011). This paternalism that developed in United Nations policy during the 1990s has a deep significance for the later policy of Responsibility to Protect.

Notwithstanding vast levels of support and cooperation within the United Nations during this period, the rise of humanitarianism within the United Nations after the Cold War was largely unsuccessful. Despite the agreement that the rights of individuals should be prioritised over the right of states to non-intervention, the enforcement of United Nations policy continued to be inconsistent, selective and dependent upon complicated networks of political power (Weiss 2012). These concerns around the effectiveness of humanitarian military intervention as an approach were exacerbated by the response of the international community to a number of humanitarian crises in the 1990s. As seen historically, the rhetoric of United Nations policy did not match its application, in reality, supporting the idea that the difference between what the United Nations claims to do and what it is actually capable of doing is heavily influenced by the political agenda of particular nations, namely the five permanent members of the Security Council.

The disillusionment with humanitarianism as a governing principle intensified following a number of events that were particularly visible in international media. The genocide in Rwanda in 1994 saw Western governments render effective international intervention impossible by not wishing to face the costs and risks associated with intervention despite the situation satisfying the agreed conditions for legitimate humanitarian intervention (Seybolt 2008). When tensions between Tutsi and Hutu populations escalated in early 1994, the United Nations peacekeeping operation present in Rwanda was severely understaffed and ill-equipped to deal with the situation (Stein 2012). As a result, despite an increased focus on the rights of individuals and widespread support for intervention on the basis of humanitarian concerns, United Nations involvement in Rwanda was unsuccessful in preventing the tragic mass murder of huge numbers of people. Indeed, in April 1994, Security Council Resolution 912 reduced the number of troops available as part of the United Nations Assistance Mission for Rwanda (UNAMIR) from 2548 to 270, making effective action impossible (Stein 2012). Despite numbers being marginally increased later on in the conflict, this particular case was heavily criticised, with many arguing that the permanent members of the Security Council could have acted sooner and prevented genocide.

The events in Kosovo in 1999 also raised concerns around the effectiveness of United Nations policies with regard to intervention. The North Atlantic Treaty Organisation (NATO) intervened in Kosovo in spite of the United Nations' inability to come to an agreement on whether or not the military intervention was appropriate. NATO's intervention in Kosovo was largely viewed as legitimate, despite not having the approval of the Security Council, existing as a case in which ethical and moral concerns were considered more significant than the approval of international law. As Stromseth et al. argue, the situation in Kosovo

> pitted fundamental human rights principles affirmed by the UN Charter against the Charter's rules limiting the resort to force – confronting NATO with the dilemma of either acting without Council authorization or tolerating severe human rights abuses in a desperate and escalating humanitarian crisis in Europe. (2006, 35)

The intervention in Kosovo was unauthorised by the Security Council due to the use of veto power by Russia and China, preventing the authorisation of the use of force, yet was seen by many as justified. These humanitarian failures, among others in the 1990s, highlight again, the ways in which United

Nations policy differs in terms of ideology and reality and the importance of viewing the activities of the Security Council through the lens of selective responsibility. The rhetoric of equality, human rights and protection seen in policy was not put into practice as a result of the institutionalised privilege of a small number of states.

These failures of humanitarianism were well publicised by news outlets around the world and prompted calls for a new approach to intervention by the international community, with existing approaches to international security being viewed as insufficient for dealing with such crises. In the case of Kosovo, the ineffectiveness of existing United Nations strategies was most clearly articulated by the international community taking action without Security Council authorisation. NATO's unauthorised bombing of Kosovo had set a precedent for bypassing United Nations policies and procedures in the name of humanitarianism, stressing the need for a new approach capable of dealing with developments in the international community if the United Nations as an institution was to continue to be relevant (Mazower 2009). The United Nations had to come up with a new approach to dealing with conflict if it was to retain its hold on international law and international relations. This call for a new approach was stated publicly by Kofi Annan, the secretary general at the time, who argued that following the number of humanitarian emergencies in the 1990s, there was a need to 'adapt our international system better to a world with new actors, new responsibilities, and new possibilities for peace and progress' (Annan 1999). Annan (1999) argued for the need to develop a system that made the issue of selectivity in interventions less likely through an understanding of intervention as being defined by and dependent upon legitimate and universal principles.

ICISS AND THE FOCUS ON RESPONSIBILITY

Following Annan's call for a new method of conducting the international intervention, the International Commission on Intervention and State Sovereignty (ICISS) was set up in 2001 to produce a report on the idea of the Responsibility to Protect and to formulate a new way for the United Nations to deal with humanitarian emergencies. The commission was made up of representatives from Australia, Algeria, Canada, the United States, Russia, Germany, South Africa, the Philippines, Switzerland, Guatemala and India. The report generated by the ICISS was voted upon and unanimously accepted at the 2005 United Nations World Summit and remains the leading principle for United Nations approaches to intervention. The resulting principle of Responsibility to Protect (also known as R2P) is ultimately a responsibility of states to their citizens, while recognising that should states fail in their duty, this becomes the responsibility of the international community more broadly.

It is possible to see within Responsibility to Protect the continued sense of paternalism that underpinned the humanitarianism of the 1990s but rebranded as a responsibility, playing on the moral connotations associated with this concept. As Rutazibwa (2010) argues, policies established by international organisations in more recent years have used an agenda of development in order to encourage a sense of moral responsibility and ethical concern within international relations. Intervention, therefore, becomes an issue of assisting 'less developed' nations on the basis of ethical and moral responsibility. Furthermore, the report of the ICISS proposed understanding sovereignty as responsibility, rather than the automatic right of a state, as well as advancing the notion that responsibility for the protection of populations ultimately lay with the state itself, but fell to the international community should a particular state fail in its duties (ICISS, 2001). Where previously the notion of sovereignty had been understood as the right of states to self-determination and the right to non-interference by the international community, the Responsibility to Protect discourse argued that sovereignty did not represent authority but responsibility for states to protect their own populations from four key crimes: genocide, war crimes, ethnic cleansing and crimes against humanity (Thakur 2006). This reconceptualisation of the notion of sovereignty implied some level of accountability on the part of states to their own people and the wider international community with regard to adherence to international human rights standards (Cohen 2012). The sovereignty of states was not to be automatically granted and respected but became dependent upon the observance of international law and human rights principles. In this way, the principle of Responsibility to Protect made the rights of states to sovereignty contingent upon the respect of the human rights of the individuals for whom that state is responsible (Bellamy 2011). It represented an extension of previous ideas of humanitarianism and the focus on human rights as the foundation of international relations while retaining criteria for legitimate intervention and emphasising the idea that intervention is only justifiable in cases of extreme abuse.

There are two brief observations worth making here in terms of the way that Responsibility to Protect reframes sovereignty without actually doing much to change the conceptualisation of sovereignty that has been implemented historically. Firstly, as Glanville (2013) explores at length, sovereignty as responsibility has a much longer history than the ICISS report and, in fact, has its roots in early modern understandings of sovereignty, but the responsibility of the international community to intervene *without consent* was new. It was the international responsibility to intervene in the domestic affairs of a state that could not or would not protect its people without the agreement of a functioning government that signified a shift in definitions of sovereignty. Secondly, this responsibility of the international community to intervene when a state fails to observe 'universal' principles as defined by the United Nations does not seem all that new either. As the earlier chapters of this book outline, this framing of sovereignty relies on the implementation of Western culture as universal culture (Grovogui 1996; Getachew 2019; Parfitt 2011). This is not to say that states ought to be able to violate the human rights of their citizens without consequence, but that the claim to universality within Responsibility to Protect and within the structures of the United Nations enables and legitimates the use of intervention as a neocolonial technology. The major powers are able to authorise intervention against the wishes of a functioning state on the basis that the state is not adhering to universal principles when there is a strong argument to say that universality privileges Western culture (Grovogui 1996).

Although Responsibility to Protect, as developed by the ICISS, elaborated on situations whereby international intervention would be appropriate, the intervention was presented as the second of three pillars, and there was also a strong focus on the idea of prevention. The ICISS report states that 'prevention is the single most important dimension of the responsibility to protect' and that the responsibility to prevent required an examination of 'both the root causes and direct causes of internal conflict and other man-made crises putting populations at risk' (ICISS 2001, XI). This focus on prevention represents an admission of the inadequacies of using intervention to deal with humanitarian emergencies and an understanding that both the state in question itself and the international community have a responsibility to intervene in a non-military manner as soon as situations of potential conflict become apparent. This was encouraged both on a moral level and a political or economic level, as prevention would address the tension between the respect of sovereignty and military intervention and be significantly less costly for intervening parties (Woocher 2012). In this sense, the ICISS encouraged a stronger feeling of the international community, encouraging assistance to failing states before situations reached the level of genocide, war crimes, ethnic cleansing or crimes against humanity. The third pillar of the responsibility to protect, as defined by the ICISS report, is the responsibility to rebuild. Should prevention fail and intervention become absolutely necessary in order to prevent large-scale harm, the international community, according to the ICISS, has a responsibility 'to provide, particularly after a military intervention, full assistance with recovery, reconstruction and reconciliation, addressing the causes of the harm the intervention was designed to halt or avert' (ICISS 2001, XI). The responsibility of the international community as suggested by the ICISS was, therefore, an extension of previous understandings of the necessity of intervention. Not only did states have a responsibility to intervene in traditional ways – militarily or otherwise – should a state be seen to be failing in its responsibilities towards its citizens, but there was also an earlier responsibility to attempt to prevent situations from escalating to the point of intervention and a later responsibility to assist in rebuilding communities following the intervention. These three pillars of the Responsibility to Protect can be clearly seen in Articles 138 and 139 of the 2005 World Summit Outcome document and became the new lens through which humanitarian assistance was viewed by the United Nations (United Nations 2005).

What lies at the heart of the responsibility promoted by the three pillars is the importance of action. The international community is deemed to have a responsibility to act when any of the four categories that constitute legitimate points for intervention – genocide, war crimes, ethnic cleansing and crimes against humanity – are met. This categorical definition of legitimate causes for intervention attempts to clarify those situations where military action is appropriate and avoid intervention under the general guise of humanitarianism, seeming to address the concerns over selective enforcement and the abuse of power within the Security Council. However, the importance of action under Responsibility to Protect is somewhat undermined by the lack of consequence for inaction, and this is the crux of the issue in understanding how selective responsibility operates. The duty to prevent, respond and rebuild is clearly articulated, but in the absence of an overall enforcing authority, there is no corresponding punishment for a *failure* to act (Welsh 2012). While individual states run the risk of intervention by the international community should they fail to live up to their responsibility to protect their own citizens, once this responsibility falls to the international community, there is no tangible consequence for their failure to live up to it. In this sense, Responsibility to Protect does not go very far in dealing with the issues associated with earlier approaches to humanitarian military intervention, namely selective enforcement and the dominance of the major powers, who can use the language of responsibility to justify intervention but face no consequences for choosing not to act upon this responsibility. As Glanville (2021) notes, responsibility is sometimes used with integrity and other times manipulated for political means, and any questions about the ethics of intervention require a consideration of the history of powerful states and their role in the 'civilizing mission'.

The issue of selective enforcement was the initial prompt for a reconceptualisation of responsibility, as outlined by Kofi Annan following the devastating events in Rwanda. The United Nations was ill-equipped to respond in Rwanda due to those member states that were capable of providing support not wishing to face the costs and risks that military action would require (Seybolt 2008). In the absence of an authority that has the power to punish inaction by those with the capacity to do so, selective enforcement of United Nations policies in this manner will continue to occur. Rather than acting on the moral obligation that is envisaged by the ICISS, states without a political interest in the outcome of conflicts make rational cost/ benefit decisions based on the likelihood of success, which raises questions around legitimacy (Murray 2012). There may be a situation that satisfies the definition of a legitimate emergency as proposed by the Responsibility to Protect principle, but there is no compelling force to action other than the sense of moral obligation seen to underpin international relations. As a result, despite the ICISS aiming to provide a structure of responsibility that would be universally applicable, we continue to see inconsistent application of the Responsibility to Protect doctrine. Furthermore, in the event that a situation is deemed a legitimate cause for action, practical issues with regard to operationalising Responsibility to Protect arise. There is no clear process for the application of Responsibility to Protect in logistical terms, and as such, the task falls to the Security Council, which has proved both incapable and unwilling to implement this policy through military intervention. Despite the ICISS' aim to provide a clear and consistent framework for intervention, the implementation of Responsibility to Protect is obstructed by issues of cost and the logistics of military deployment, such as chains of command (Murray 2012).

In its early days, the principle of Responsibility to Protect suffered a number of blows to its reputation following these issues of global power relations, particularly at the hands of the British government under Tony Blair and the US government under George W. Bush. Following its founding by the ICISS in 2001, the language of Responsibility to Protect was used heavily by the US and British governments to retroactively – and inaccurately – justify their involvement in the invasion of Iraq (Chalk et al. 2012). The use of this framework to defend the Iraq invasion subsequently damaged the reputation of Responsibility to Protect following the intensely negative public response, emphasising the way in which constructions of responsibility with regards to human rights are heavily influenced by power and the capacity for particular actors to appropriate discourse to justify their actions. The aftermath of the Iraq invasion, particularly in relation to the atrocities of Abu Ghraib, meant that the US government was no longer viewed as a guarantor of international rights. Following this, Responsibility to Protect was viewed with cynicism by a number of actors in the international community, who saw it as another potential framework for neocolonial dominance by the world's most powerful. The lack of power that the United Nations has – despite its authority – meant that the global hegemonic powers remained immune to punishment (Mahdavi 2012). These concerns were stressed particularly by Arab and Asian states following the 2005 World Summit, who came to view Responsibility to Protect as a reconceptualisation of humanitarian intervention, providing the opportunity for coercive interference in the domestic affairs of states (Bellamy 2011).

These concerns around the relationship between Responsibility to Protect as a means of human protection and other political goals, such as regime change, have retained significance in recent years, particularly within the context of the Middle East and North Africa (Bellamy and Williams 2011). The end of 2010 saw the beginnings of revolutionary protests across the Middle East and North Africa, and following an escalating conflict between the Gaddafi government and rebel forces, the United Nations Security Council adopted Resolution 1973 on 17 March 2011, authorising international forces to use 'all necessary measures' to protect Libyan civilians (United Nations 2011). This was not the first time that Responsibility to Protect had been used in order to authorise intervention, but its significance stood in the fact that United Nations involvement was not welcomed by the Gaddafi regime. Resolution 1973 was the first instance of Responsibility to Protect being used to justify intervention and the use of force *against the wishes of a functioning state* (Bellamy and Williams 2011). The Libyan case was also the first example of Responsibility to Protect being used in the Middle East and Northern Africa (Mahdavi 2012). The United Nations' response to the conflict in Libya, therefore, represented an unfamiliar use of policy around intervention and the idea of responsibility than had been seen before. It was the most severe application of Responsibility to Protect that had been seen.

The intervention in Libya saw concerns raised specifically around the relationship between Responsibility to Protect, and the political goal of regime change within the international community, with critics arguing that while intervention with the aim of protecting human life is legitimate, intervention with the basic political aim of regime change is not (Bellamy and Williams 2011). This particular case draws attention to the way in which those nations with the most political power, namely the five permanent members of the Security Council, are able to appropriate United Nations policy in order to justify and legitimate intervention with potentially political rather than humanitarian aims and objectives. This was of particular significance in the case of Libya, as the larger narrative of the Arab Spring protests was the claim that these countries wished to transcend the West rather than replicate it, rejecting colonial and postcolonial oppression (Dabashi 2012). The very purpose of the revolutions across the Middle East and North Africa was independence and freedom for civilians, both from a dictatorial regime and their continued economic exploitation by the West. Instead, they received further oppression through a military intervention that sought to ensure the perpetuation of postcolonial structures of power.

The Security Council discussions around intervention received significant media coverage at the time, highlighting the tensions between East and West that escalated in 2016 in relation to Syria, seeming to have revived the Cold War frictions between the United States and Russia in particular. This tension appeared to be brewing in the Security Council during the immediate aftermath of the Libyan intervention. The revolutionary protests in Libya spread to Syria in the later months of 2011. Despite similarities between the two contexts, a draft proposal for intervention in Syria put forward by the UK, France, Germany and Portugal was not accepted by the Security Council. Both Russia and China vetoed the proposals, with Russia explicitly citing the Western 'betrayal' over Libya as their reason for doing so (Rotmann et al. 2014, 368). While Responsibility to Protect was implemented in response to the conflict in Libya based on protecting the lives of civilians where their government had failed to do so, the Russian government deemed the response of the international community as something that amounted to more than protection or humanitarian relief. To date, Russia and China have vetoed ten draft resolutions for action in Syria, citing the principle of non-interference (Kul 2022). In initial debates around Syria, the Russian government argued that the air strikes that formed a part of the military intervention in Libya were not consistent with the protection of civilians but rather represented support for anti-government forces in order to topple the Gaddafi regime that had fallen out of favour with British and American governments (Averre and Davies 2015). As such, the Russian government has remained absolute in its stance and consistently prevented action by the United Nations in Syria. While this is undoubtedly in part due to the political relationship between the Russian and Syrian governments, the defiance of the Russian government is also representative of a Cold War attitude towards the West, signifying a clear statement that Russia will not be overruled by British and American political desires and a clear objection to the disregard of the principle of non-intervention as respect for the right of states to sovereign authority (Averre and Davies 2015). The concept of selective responsibility pushes us to question the United Nations' continued reliance on discourses of responsibility in light of inconsistent application and selective enforcement of Responsibility to Protect in recent years, and emphasises the extent to which issues of global political power infiltrate international relations.

As Bellamy (2022) argues, Responsibility to Protect is a norm, an expectation of behaviour, but the problem lies in the fact that the United Nations is political, not judicial. It has the capacity to create norms but no legal basis for enforcing them. While authority represents the capacity to create norms and provide them with legitimacy as the result of a political process, as with the United Nations, power relates to the capacity to enforce these norms (Thakur 2006). It follows that although the United Nations has the authority to create norms such as Responsibility to Protect and provide them with legitimacy through an international political process, the lack of a binding contract to action means that they are dependent on the world's strongest military powers to enforce these norms. In other words, as was seen in Libya and Syria, the United Nations is unable to enforce its authority with regard to the Responsibility to Protect without the support of the five permanent members of the Security Council. However, Bellamy (2022) also contends that Responsibility to Protect cannot be deemed a 'failure' on this basis. Rather, we must consider the response to its implementation or non-implementation as a means of establishing a shared sense of appropriate behaviour. If, as was the case for Syria, the international community responds critically to non-implementation, it demonstrates a shared vision for appropriate behaviour that reinforces Responsibility to Protect as a norm (Bellamy 2022).

Although Responsibility to Protect makes appeals to a moral obligation and a sense of common humanity, the reality is that action remains constrained by the unequal power relations in global politics. It is naive to think that these powerful states will act purely in the utopian interests of common humanity. Their decisions are always influenced by rational understandings of the costs and benefits, both financial and political, involved in intervening based on the Responsibility to Protect. Powerful states are motivated by self-interest, demonstrating the fragility of Responsibility to Protect as a norm (Eskiduman 2022). As with previous approaches to international relations and humanitarian interventions, Responsibility to Protect becomes a question of power and the capacity to perform this responsibility selectively. Powerful states may, through the United Nations, intervene in the name of protecting the rights of minorities suffering from human rights abuses, but there is no corresponding protection for the weak against the dominant international moral majority (Thakur 2006). Responsibility to Protect, in this sense, runs the risk of legitimating a particular understanding of progress and the enforcement of a singular conception of moral values. Selective enforcement will continue to be an issue for as long as the United Nations as a world organisation relies upon the cooperation of the world's major powers.

The main issue arising from this conception of responsibility is that of collective action. Responsibility to Protect is based on an understanding of a unified international community that has a collective responsibility to protect, both at the individual level of states to their own people and the global level. In reality, this international community is a complex network of power relations (Mahdavi 2012). The capacity for action is dependent upon the cooperation of the world's most powerful states, without whom the international community, in the sense of capacity for collective action, ceases to exist. The United Nations Security Council cannot be viewed as the agent of enforcement with regards to moral responsibility as its success or failure to live up to this responsibility is dependent upon the action of member states, who are left to make a judgement call based on competing priorities (Glanville 2021). The emphasis of Responsibility to Protect on a collective moral responsibility fails to recognise these fundamental issues of power, instead choosing to believe that states will act in the interests of common humanity as members of an international community. As Knight states, with regards to implementing the Responsibility to Protect, 'to assign this task to the "international community" is to assign the task to everyone and no one' (2012, 283). The current global order and organisation of state boundaries do not allow for collective action in this way. Assigning the task of protection to the international community provides a number of potential rescuers and, as a result, less chance of actual rescue (Welsh 2012). Thus, despite initial optimism with regards to Responsibility to Protect and its potential to provide a more transparent and concrete framework for dealing with acts of genocide, war crimes, ethnic cleansing and crimes against humanity, a number of questions and concerns remain about the use of moral claims to responsibility in order to legitimate dominance and perpetuate the existing global order. Selective enforcement and the lack of consequence for inaction continue to thwart the consistent application of the principle in dealing with humanitarian emergencies. The conflicts arising in the Middle East and North Africa in recent years have highlighted the extent to which national interests always trump humanitarian needs (Hehir 2016).

Twenty years of Responsibility to Protect has, however, seen scholars reflect on its effectiveness and propose ways in which the issue of selectivity could be overcome. Unsurprisingly, the consensus is that reliance on the Security Council is the primary issue, particularly while the permanent members retain their right to veto. Within this framework, the Security Council decides who is worth saving, and their decisions have proved to be inconsistent and prejudiced (Eskiduman 2022). Given that Security Council reform is unlikely to be imminent, where the Security Council is unable to implement Responsibility to Protect, states could expand their settlement schemes for refugees, which as Glanville (2021) notes, would be a test of their sincerity. If states were truly acting in the interests of protecting innocent civilians, their immigration and resettlement policies would reflect this. Instead, refugees are most likely to be resettled in neighbouring countries, despite the strain this puts on global south states (Kul 2022). Thakur (2018) has also emphasised the need to engage emerging powers in developing the criteria for Responsibility to Protect, while Šimonović (2019) argues that we ought to focus on the practicalities of implementation rather than conceptual debate. All of these assessments of Responsibility to Protect retain a commitment to protecting innocent civilians and strengthening the capacity of the

United Nations to act in cases of humanitarian emergency. Undoubtedly, the international community should act in these circumstances, but this book has shown that the United Nations as an organisation and its utilisation of responsibility as a concept is problematic in that it reproduces the power dynamics of colonialism.

NEOCOLONIALISM AND SELECTIVE RESPONSIBILITY

This chapter perhaps seems out of place within the context of a book on the history of the United Nations and anti-colonial resistance to it. The purpose of providing this brief history of the development of policies on intervention within the context of the United Nations is to emphasise the importance of telling accurate histories on the basis that these histories enable and shape our present. This chapter has shown the stark contrast between initial commitments to non-intervention by the United Nations and later principle of the Responsibility to Protect, which amounts to a moral duty to intervene in the affairs of other states. To be explicit, the argument that has been developed here is that Responsibility to Protect signifies the latest stage in the historical domination of particular parts of the world by others and that it functions as a neocolonial technology of power that legitimates the dominance of the major powers through continued reliance on the hierarchical understanding of global society that has been institutionalised in the United Nations. Sovereignty under Responsibility to Protect is no longer the right to self-determination but is a capacity that states have depended upon their adherence to Western cultural norms (Rutazibwa 2014). As we have seen continuously throughout history, cultural difference is unable to be understood purely as differences within this framework. Instead, all non-Western states are dealt with through the ideologies of development and progress, whereby their difference needs to be eradicated and their culture assimilated, usually by force (Rutazibwa 2014). This is emphasised through the continued process – that we have seen throughout the history of sovereignty as a concept – of making sovereignty contingent upon submission to terms decided by the West. As argued throughout this book, sovereignty for non-European states has always been dependent upon adherence to Western values, and we continue to see this within the context of Responsibility to Protect and the reconceptualisation of sovereignty as responsibility.

Following the formal decolonisation of the majority of the world, Responsibility to Protect serves as a neocolonial policy, providing major powers with the right to intervene – or not intervene – when and where they deem it appropriate while simultaneously removing the rights of former colonies to non-intervention as outlined in the Charter of the United Nations. The purpose of the argument developed throughout this chapter is not to suggest that the sovereignty of violent dictatorial governments should be prioritised over the lives of civilians but rather to disturb dominant understandings of the United Nations and particularly the Security Council as acting in the interests of international peace and security. This chapter illustrates to material consequences of a structure that enables selective responsibility. The issue of selectivity provides a clear example of the way in which neocolonialism functions within the contemporary practices of the United Nations, and as Nkrumah argues, 'Neo-colonialism is the worst form of imperialism. For those who practice it, it means power without responsibility and for those who suffer from it, it means exploitation without redress' (1965, xi). Through the Responsibility to Protect, the United Nations seeks to perpetuate colonial power relations while claiming to be acting in the interests of freedom.

The ability of the major powers to continue to manipulate policy in their interests in spite of more recent attempts to restrain this control highlights the magnitude of their privilege within the United Nations. In this chapter, the intervention has been used as an example of how postcolonial power manifests in reality through neocolonial mechanisms, as well as being an illustration of the importance of understanding the historical context of contemporary debates. The reconceptualisation of sovereignty as responsibility serves to legitimate the existing global order and justify intervention that is often politically motivated. Furthermore, the language of responsibility that is used in framing the policy seeks to legitimise the United Nations as an organisation committed to peace, but the structure of the organisation and the lack of consequence for a failure to implement the policy allows Western powers to distance themselves from any real sense of responsibility (Chandler 2010). Ultimately, even when the policy makes clear the circumstances under which intervention is appropriate and necessary, it is still within the power of the permanent five members of the Security Council to enforce this policy, and there is no consequence for their failure to do so (Welsh 2012). As such, this policy functions to justify the interventions the major powers do decide to undertake as the actions of world leaders who are responsible for the protection of civilians suffering abuse at the hands of their own governments, while failing to compel these same world leaders to act in all cases that meet the criteria for intervention. The contemporary examples that have been utilised in this chapter related to the uprisings in the Middle East and North Africa emphasise the degree to which this policy has failed to address selectivity and the power of the permanent members of the Security Council to continue to manipulate the organisation in line with their own political interests. Evidently, the United Nations will continue to act selectively in cases of civil war and humanitarian emergency while the structure of the organisation remains unchanged. As long as its permanent members and their ability to veto dominate the Security Council, selectivity will be inevitable. Providing a historical narrative of the development from non-intervention to a responsibility to intervene shows how, at different periods in time, the United Nations has been able to maintain systems of colonial and neocolonial domination and perpetuate global hierarchies of power that were established by colonialism. Each of these approaches to intervention following formal decolonisation has allowed for the continuation of selective enforcement of interventionist policy in line with major power interests, which has been justified through the language of responsibility and ideologies of development and civilisation.

Conclusion

This book began with a question: How is it possible that two humanitarian crises, in the same region and at the same time, saw such wildly different responses from the international community? How was a full-scale military intervention authorised in Libya within months while there have been ten years of inaction in Syria? On one level, the answer is quite simple. The United Nations, as the primary international organisation for maintaining peace and security, is dominated by five of the world's most powerful states, and they ultimately make a cost/benefit analysis when deciding whether or not to intervene. However, reading this debate through history provides a much more complex picture, and focusing on the question of responsibility forces us to reckon with the colonial history of the United Nations.

As discussed in chapter 6, decisions around intervention within the United Nations have, since 2001, fallen under the policy of Responsibility to Protect. This policy was imagined as a means of preventing humanitarian emergencies in the first instance but to provide clearer guidelines and criteria for an international response (ICISS 2001). Responsibility here refers to the responsibility of states to their own populations first and foremost, but also a broader responsibility of the international community via the United Nations to protect people at risk of human rights violations. The argument of this book is that the continued reliance on responsibility as a way of mediating international relations reproduces the power dynamics of colonialism and Eurocentrism. The concept of *selective responsibility* utilised here pushes us to think critically about the problematic discourses that underpin the framework of responsibility within the United Nations. With this in mind, the aim of this book has been twofold: firstly, to disturb the dominant narratives of equality and progress that surround the United Nations and that present the power dynamics inherent in this framework of responsibility as natural; and secondly, to reconstruct these narratives in order to account for the role of colonialism and a long history of anti-colonial activism that has been marginalised. Here, I will pull together some of the key arguments of the book and its implications for how we understand the contemporary activities of the United Nations.

SELECTIVE RESPONSIBILITY

Throughout this book, the concept of selective responsibility has served as a prompt to think about the historical structures than enable the selective enforcement of policy within the United Nations. While the United Nations itself seeks to present responsibility as a neutral, objective and humanitarian principle, the argument here is that Responsibility to Protect as a policy is neocolonial in nature. It enables the permanent members of the Security Council to take or prevent action that serves their own interests politically and economically, and over the last twenty years we have seen frequent manipulations of the discourse of responsibility to this effect (Glanville 2021). Reframing this as *selective* responsibility illuminates the ways in which the very structures of the United Nations facilitate the execution of postcolonial and neocolonial power.

Underpinning selective responsibility within the United Nations are discourses of development and progress that view the world through a Eurocentric hierarchy, and the centrality of sovereignty as a principle is key to this. As the chapters of this book have demonstrated, sovereignty has been used historically to instil and reproduce hierarchy in the international arena (Getachew 2019; Parfitt 2011). It is not an objective status assigned to states but rather developed in conjunction with colonialism as a means of justifying colonial domination (Anghie 2001, 2005). European states considered themselves sovereign and justified colonialism as a process by which non-European states could become sovereign. Within this framework, non-European states could *become* sovereign through adherence to European values, which were construed as universal values (Grovogui 1996). Colonialism, therefore, generated a hierarchy of sovereignties, which chapter 2 explores in significant detail. Closely linked to this is the discourse of development, which sees non-European states as existing in an earlier stage of civilisation and in need of tutelage by 'more advanced' nations (Patil 2008). It is these racialised colonial logics that underpin ideas of responsibility within international relations and have been entrenched within international institutions.

It follows that responsibility *itself* is a problematic concept, as it relies on a worldview grounded in racialised inequality and Eurocentrism. If we accept that the concept of responsibility within this context is problematic as a consequence of its colonial origins, the task for contemporary scholars becomes less about identifying strategies for strengthening responsibility within the United Nations and more about addressing the economic, political and social structures that reproduce the inequalities of colonialism. The United Nations' continued reliance on responsibility as a justification for the privilege of the permanent members of the Security Council serves only to reproduce these colonial power dynamics. Furthermore, in the absence of an overarching authority that would enforce this responsibility, it will always be applied selectively.

The archival material examined throughout this book has provided an alternative narrative to the dominant history of the United Nations as an organisation grounded in equality. From the League against Imperialism to the Group of 77, non-Western actors have challenged and questioned the dominance of the major powers within international institutions on the basis of a burden of responsibility. While a close reading of these movements has highlighted their complexities, diversity and internal conflicts, they have all, in one way or another, provided alternative visions for a global society. The League against Imperialism emphasised the contradictions of an organisation making claims to self-determination while maintaining colonial rule, while anti-colonial activists at San Francisco sought to get decolonisation on the agenda and raised concerns over the structure of the Security Council. Bandung cultivated solidarities and partnerships between Asian and African states, utilising the political context of the Cold War to push decolonisation onto the agenda at the United Nations, and more recent groups such as the Non-Aligned Movement and Group of 77 have, despite internal conflicts, continued to hold the United Nations to account on matters of political and economic inequality. These archives provide a starting point for challenging the dominance of the major powers and thinking about what an alternative might look like.

The purpose of reading these contemporary issues around intervention through this history of anti-colonialism is to challenge Eurocentrism, both in our political institutions and in the stories we tell of them. Eurocentrism refers to the often taken-for-granted idea that Europe is economically, politically and culturally distinctive, and that the European model is, or ought to be, universal (Sabaratnam 2017; Grovogui 1996). The focus here on constructing an alternative narrative is intended to show that the dominant narrative reinforces Eurocentrism and so reproduces the power dynamics inherent in Eurocentrism and to provide an example that emphasises the importance of listening to the counter-discourses that are often obscured by claims that Western history represents universal history (Morefield 2014).

INTERNATIONAL RELATIONS, HISTORY AND EUROCENTRISM

The debates examined here lead to three primary conclusions in terms of the broader implications for international relations. Firstly, that the international relations scholarship needs to do more to address the ongoing consequences of colonialism in relation to international institutions. This must go beyond telling stories of a concurrent but separate history and instead reconstruct our understandings of the modern world, challenging the naturalisation of inequality on a global scale. Revisiting and remembering historical events is not only about establishing the inaccuracies of existing narratives but reconstructing them (Grovogui 2016). This allows us to question the structure of the organisation that claims to recognise the sovereign equality of all states and view questions of responsibility within the United Nations through a different lens. Rather than focusing only on how power is exercised in current international conflicts, we must address the historical conditions that make the exercise of this power possible and that, in many cases, have significance for the economic, political and social foundations of these conflicts in the first instance. In the specific case of Responsibility to Protect, identifying the historical conditions that made possible the institutionalisation of great power privilege provides a clearer understanding of how selective responsibility operates in the present day.

Secondly, addressing the Eurocentrism of international relations requires a recognition of the fact that politics happens outside of the West and this can provide us with alternative possibilities for solidarities both between non-Western states and between the West and non-West (Sabaratnam 2017). A revitalisation of anti-colonial spirit such as that seen at Bandung and other organisations or movements generates more than a historical record of earlier solidarities. It leads us not only to a different understanding of what the United Nations is, in that it demonstrates the extent to which these states were subject to neocolonialism, but also a different understanding of what the United Nations *could be*. It provides innovative proposals for governing relationships between states economically, politically and socially while addressing and repairing the damage done by colonialism.

Finally, the accuracy of historical narratives is important and has implications for our understanding of the present, especially (but not only) in relation to international institutions. Re-narrating the history of the United Nations is important not only to understand the facts of what happened but also to better understand the power structures that enable and legitimate particular activities in the present. It changes our understanding from one of the exercise of power broadly speaking to the exercise of a particular type of power – that is, colonial or neocolonial power. In the case of intervention, for example, the authorisation of intervention and the overriding of the right of states to govern within their own borders without intervention is often seen as the exercise of power by states who are powerful (economically, politically and militarily). Reading these debates through a colonial history shows that intervention is part of a much longer process of control and domination that is not only about military power but also about reinforcing Eurocentric ideologies around progress, development and what it means to be civilized. Re-narrating the history of the United Nations, taking into account the ideas and critiques of anti-colonial movements, alters our understanding of these activities.

This book contributes to a broader body of work that seeks to challenge the Eurocentrism of international relations scholarship and recognise the historical contributions of political actors from around the globe. As Phạm and Shilliam argue:

Peoples in the so-called Third World or Global South have been continually treated as objects, usually of interventions and are rarely conceived as co-authors of and in international relations, who collectively practice their own visions of political order and just relations. (2016, 17–18)

The archival documents used here demonstrate that these anti-colonial activists are political actors, contesting historical narratives that frame non-Western states and peoples as 'backwards' and in need of tutelage from 'more developed' states. This provides a challenge to the concept of responsibility that features heavily in United Nations rhetoric that justifies the continued dominance of the major powers within international relations. The tradition of postcolonial theory highlights the consequences of a continued acceptance of the idea that modernity began in Europe as a result of European enlightenment and innovation, whereby Western liberalism is the end point for all.

THE UNITED NATIONS IN 2022

In concluding, I want to briefly turn to the question of the role of the United Nations in 2022. While this book, on the whole, has painted a fairly pessimistic picture of the United Nations and its capacities, it is worth noting that the focus here has primarily been on the role of the Security Council and the question of intervention. Beyond the Security Council, various other organs of the United Nations do important work in more collaborative ways, and so this is not to say that the United Nations should be disbanded wholesale. Rather, this book has sought to call into question the power dynamics entrenched in the organisation – particularly within the Security Council – and the colonial discourses that legitimise them. The archival material examined here has demonstrated that gains have been made via the General Assembly and that non-Western states continue to seek reform of the United Nations rather than its abolition. The argument sustained here, however, is that reform needs to go beyond voting and participation to deal with the ideological underpinnings of the organisation or we will continue to see the major powers enact selective responsibility.

Recent years have seen rising tensions within historic disagreements between the permanent members of the Security Council, particularly on questions of intervention. As outlined in chapter 6, Russia and China have consistently invoked their right to veto with the aim of preventing intervention on the grounds of a commitment to non-interference (Kul 2022; Glanville 2013). And yet, at the time of writing, the United Nations is in crisis as a result of the Russian invasion of Ukraine. The General Assembly has voted to suspend Russia from the Human Rights Council on the basis that they have committed 'gross and systematic violations of human rights' (United Nations, 2022b). That one of the permanent five members of the Security Council could be responsible for breaches of international peace and security rather than protecting it only serves to reinforce the hypocrisy of an organisation ordered around the particular responsibility of these five states.

Bibliography

SECONDARY SOURCES

Acharya, Amitav and See Seng Tan (2008) 'The Normative Relevance of the Bandung Conference for Contemporary Asian and International Order' in Amitav Acharya and See Seng Tan (Eds.), *Bandung Revisited: The Legacy of the 1955 Asian-African Conference for International Order*, Singapore: NUS Press, pp. 1–18.

Alden, Chris; Morphet, Sally and Vieira, Marco Antonio (2010) *The South in World Politics*, Basingstoke: Palgrave Macmillan.

Anand, R.P. (2010) 'The Formation of International Organizations and India: A Historical Study', *Leiden Journal of International Law*, Volume 23, Number 1, pp. 5–21.

Anderson, Carol (1996) 'From Hope to Disillusion: African Americans, the United Nations, and the Struggle for Human Rights', *Diplomatic History*, Volume 20, Number 4, pp. 531–563.

Anderson, Carol (2003) *Eyes off the Prize: The United Nations and the African American Struggle for Human Rights, 1944–1955*, Cambridge: Cambridge University Press.

Anderson, Carol (2015) *Bourgeois Radicals: The NAACP and the Struggle for Colonial Liberation*, Cambridge: Cambridge University Press.

Anghie, Antony (2001) 'Colonialism and the Birth of International Institutions: Sovereignty, Economy, and the Mandate System of the League of Nations', *Journal of International Law and Politics*, Volume 34, pp. 513–633.

Anghie, Antony (2005) *Imperialism, Sovereignty and the Making of International Law*, Cambridge: Cambridge University Press.

Anghie, Antony (2014) 'Towards a Postcolonial International Law' in Prabhakar Singh and Benoit Mayer (Eds.), *Critical International Law: Postrealism, Postcolonialism and Transnationalism*, Oxford: Oxford University Press, pp. 123–142.

Annan, Kofi (1999) 'Two Concepts of Sovereignty', *The Economist*; 16 September 1999, Available online: http://www.economist.com/node/324795 Accessed 12 April 2022.

Archer, Clive (1992) *International Organizations* (2nd Edition), London: Routledge.

Averre, Derek and Lance Davies (2015) 'Russia, Humanitarian Intervention and the Responsibility to Protect: the Case of Syria', *International Affairs*, Volume 91, Number 4, pp. 813–834.

Baehr, Peter R. and Leon Gordenker (2005) *The United Nations: Reality and Ideal*, Basingstoke: Palgrave Macmillan.

Barnett, Michael (2002) *Eyewitness to a Genocide: The United Nations and Rwanda*, New York: Cornell University Press.

Barnett, Michael (2011) *The Empire of Humanity: A History of Humanitarianism*, New York: Cornell University Press.

Bellamy, Alex (2022) 'Sovereignty Redefined: The Promise and Practice of R2P' in Pinar Gözen Ercan (Ed.), *The Responsibility to Protect Twenty Years On: Rhetoric and Implementation*, Cham: Palgrave Macmillan.

Bellamy, Alex and Paul Williams (2011) 'The New Politics of Protection: Cote d'Ivoire, Libya and the Responsibility to Protect', *International Affairs*, Volume 87, Number 4, pp. 825–850.

Bertrand, Maurice (1995) 'The UN as an Organization: A Critique of its Functioning', *European Journal of International Law*, Volume 6, Number 3, pp. 349–359.

Bhabha, Homi (1994) *The Location of Culture*, Abingdon: Routledge.

Bhambra, Gurminder K. (2007) *Rethinking Modernity: Postcolonialism and the Sociological Imagination*, Basingstoke: Palgrave Macmillan.

Bhambra, Gurminder K. and Robbie Shilliam (2009) 'Introduction: "Silence" and Human Rights' in Gurminder K. Bhambra and Robbie Shilliam (Eds.), *Silencing Human Rights: Critical Engagements with a Contested Project*, Basingstoke: Palgrave Macmillan, pp. 1–15.

Birn, Donald S. (1981) *The League of Nations Union 1918-1945*, Oxford: Clarendon Press.

Blackburn, Robin (2010) 'Reclaiming Human Rights', *New Left Review*, Volume 69, June 2011, pp. 126–138.

Bosco, David L. (2009) *Five to Rule Them All: The UN Security Council and the Making of the Modern World*, Oxford: Oxford University Press.

Bruckenhaus, Daniel (2017) *Policing Transnational Protest: Liberal Imperialism and the Surveillance of Anti-colonialists in Europe, 1905–1945*, New York: Oxford University Press.

Çakmak, Cenap (2019) 'The United Nations and the Arab Spring' in Cenap Çakmak and Ali Onur Özçelik (Eds.), *The World Community and the Arab Spring*, Cham: Palgrave Macmillan, pp. 17–39.

Chakrabarty, Dipesh (2010) 'The Legacies of Bandung: Decolonization and the Politics of Culture' in Christopher J. Lee (Ed.), *Making a World After Empire: The Bandung Moment and Its Political Afterlives*, Athens: Ohio University Press.

Chalk, Frank, Romeo Dallaire and Kyle Matthews (2012) 'The Responsibility to React' in W. Andy Knight and Frazer Egerton (Eds.), *The Routledge Handbook of the Responsibility to Protect*, Abingdon: Routledge, pp. 36–49.

Chandler, David (2010) 'R2P or Not R2P? More Statebuilding, Less Responsibility', *Global Responsibility to Protect 2*, pp. 161–166.

Churchill, Winston and Franklin D. Roosevelt (1941) 'The Atlantic Charter', Available online: http://www.nato.int/cps/en/natolive/official_texts_16912.htm. Accessed 12 April 2022.

Churchill, Winston, Franklin D. Roosevelt and Joseph Stalin (1943) 'Declaration of the Three Powers, December 1, 1943', Available online: https://avalon.law.yale.edu/wwii/tehran.asp. Accessed 12 April 2022.

Cohen, Roberta (2012) 'From Sovereign Responsibility to R2P' in W. Andy Knight and Frazer Egerton (Eds.), *The Routledge Handbook of the Responsibility to Protect*, Abingdon: Routledge, pp. 7–21.

Dabashi, Hamid (2012) *The Arab Spring: The End of Postcolonialism*, London: Zed Books.

Diamond, Sara (2005) 'African Academy of Arts and Research' in Nina Mjagkij (Ed.), *Organizing Black America: An Encyclopedia of African American Associations*, New York: Taylor and Francis, pp. 2–3.

Dinkel, Jürgen (2019) *The Non-Aligned Movement: Genesis, Organization and Politics (1927–1992)*, Boston: Lieden.

Donaldson, Megan (2020) 'The League of Nations, Ethiopia, and the Making of States', *Humanity: An International Journal of Human Rights, Humanitarianism, and Development*, Volume 11, Number 1, pp. 6–31.

Doty, Roxanne Lynn (1996) *Imperial Encounters: The Politics of Representation in North-South Relations*, Minneapolis: University of Minnesota Press.

Douzinas, Costas (2007) *Human Rights and Empire: The Political Philosophy of Cosmopolitanism*, Abingdon: Routledge Cavendish.

Doyle, Michael and Nicholas Sambanis (2006) *Making War and Building Peace: United Nations Peace Operations*, Princeton: Princeton University Press.

Eskiduman, Özgecan (2022) 'Gaza: R2P and Selective Implementation' in Pinar Gözen Ercan (Ed.), *The Responsibility to Protect Twenty Years On: Rhetoric and Implementation*, Cham: Palgrave Macmillan.

Fanon, Frantz (1967) *The Wretched of the Earth*, London: Penguin

Fassbender, Bardo and Anne Peters (2012) 'Introduction: Towards a Global Theory of International Law' in Bardo Fassbender and Anne Peters (Eds.), *The Oxford Handbook of the History of International Law*, Oxford: Oxford University Press, pp. 1–24.

Fine, Robert (2007) *Cosmopolitanism*, Oxford: Routledge.

Foucault, Michel (2002 [1972]) *Archaeology of Knowledge*, Abingdon: Routledge.

Fox, William T.R. (1946) 'The Super-Powers at San Francisco', *The Review of Politics*, Volume 8, Number 1, pp. 115–127.

Gandhi, Leela (1998) *Postcolonial Theory: A Critical Introduction*, Edinburgh: Edinburgh University Press.

Getachew, Adom (2019) *Worldmaking after Empire: The Rise and Fall of Self Determination*, New Jersey: Princeton University Press.

Gilchrist, Huntington (1945) 'Colonial Questions at the San Francisco Conference', *The American Political Science Review*, Volume 39, Number 5, pp. 982–992.

Glanville, Luke (2013) *Sovereignty and the Responsibility to Protect: A New History*, Chicago: University of Chicago Press.

Glanville, Luke (2021) *Sharing Responsibility: The History and Future of Protection from Atrocities*, Princeton: Princeton University Press.

Goebel, Michael (2015) *Anti-Imperial Metropolis: Interwar Paris and the Seeds of Third World Nationalism*, Cambridge: Cambridge University Press.

Goodrich, Leland M. (1959) *The United Nations*, London: Stevens and Sons Ltd.

Goodwin, Geoffrey L. (1971) 'The United Nations: Expectations and Experience' in Kenneth J. Twitchett (Ed.), *The Evolving United Nations: A Prospect for Peace*, London: Europa Publications Ltd, pp. 28–56.

Grant, Kevin (2007) 'Human Rights and Sovereign Abolitions of Slavery, c. 1855–1956' in Kevin Grant, Philippa Levine and Frank Trentmann (Eds.), *Beyond Sovereignty: Britain, Empire and Transnationalism C. 1880 1950*, Basingstoke: Palgrave Macmillan, pp. 80–102.

Grovogui, Siba N. (1996) *Sovereigns, Quasi Sovereigns, and Africans: Race and Self-Determination in International Law*, Minneapolis: University of Minnesota Press.

Grovogui, Siba N. (2016) 'Remembering Bandung: When the Streams Crested, Tidal Waves Formed, and an Estuary Appeared' in Phạm, Quỳnh N. and Robbie Shilliam (Eds.), (2016) *Meanings of Bandung: Postcolonial Orders and Decolonial Visions*, London: Rowman and Littlefield.

Haas, Ernst B. (2009) 'The Attempt to Terminate Colonialism: Acceptance of the United Nations Trusteeship System', *International Organization*, Volume 7, Number 1, pp. 1–21.

Hehir, Adrian (2016) 'Assessing the Influence of the Responsibility to Protect on the UN Security Council During the Arab Spring', *Cooperation and Conflict*, Volume 51, Number 2, pp. 166–183.

Higgins, Rosalyn (1995) 'Peace and Security: Achievements and Failures', *European Journal of International Law*, Volume 6, Number 3, pp. 445–460.

Hilderbrand, Robert (1990) *Dumbarton Oaks: The Origins of the United Nations and the Search for Postwar Security*, Chapel Hill: University of North Carolina Press.

Hurd, Ian (2007) *After Anarchy: Legitimacy and Power in the United Nations Security Council*, Princeton: Princeton University Press.

Isaac A. Kamola and Shiera S. el-Malik (2017) 'Introduction: Politics of African Anticolonial Archive' in Shiera S. el-Malik and Isaac A. Kamola (Eds.), *Politics of African Anticolonial Archive*, London: Rowman and Littlefield International.

Jones, Branwen Gruffydd (2017) 'Comradeship, Committed and Conscious: The Anticolonial Archive Speaks to Our Times' in Shiera S. el-Malik and Isaac A. Kamola (Eds.), *Politics of African Anticolonial Archive*, London: Rowman and Littlefield International.

Jones, Lee (2013) 'Sovereignty, Intervention, and Social Order in Revolutionary Times', *Review of International Studies*, Volume 39, Number 5, pp. 1149–1167.

Kaldor, Mary (2003) *Global Civil Society*, Cambridge: Polity.

Kanwar, Vik (2017) 'Not a Place, but a Project' in Luis Eslava, Michael Fakhri and Vasuki Nesiah (Eds.), *Bandung, Global History, and International Law*, Cambridge: Cambridge University Press, pp. 140–158.

Kennedy, Paul (2006) *The Parliament of Man*, London: Penguin.

Knight, W. Andy (2012) 'Concluding Thoughts' in W. Andy Knight and Frazer Egerton (Eds.), The Routledge Handbook of the Responsibility to Protect, Abingdon: Routledge, pp. 276–283.

Koskenniemi, Martti (2005) 'International Law in Europe: Between Tradition and Renewal', *The European Journal of International Law*, Volume 16, Number 1, pp. 113–124.

Krasner, Stephen (2009) *Power, the State and Sovereignty: Essays on International Relations*, New York: Routledge.

Krisch, Nico (2008) 'The Security Council and the Great Powers' in Vaughan Lowe, Adam Roberts, Jennifer Welsh and Dominik Zaum (Eds.), *The United Nations Security Council and War: The Evolution of Thought and Practice Since 1945*, Oxford: Oxford University Press, pp. 133–153.

Kul, Selin (2022) 'Libya and Syria: The Protection of Refugees and R2P' in Pinar Gözen Ercan (Ed.), *The Responsibility to Protect Twenty Years On: Rhetoric and Implementation*, Cham: Palgrave Macmillan.

Lauren, Paul Gordon (2003) 'Seen from the Outside: The International Perspective on America's Dilemma' in Brenda Plummer (Ed.), *Window on Freedom: Race, Civil Rights and Foreign Affairs, 1945–1988*, Chapel Hill: University of North Carolina Press, pp. 21–43.

Lee, Christopher (2010) 'Introduction: Between a Moment and an Era: The Origins and Afterlives of Bandung' in Christopher Lee (Ed.), *Making a World After Empire: The Bandung Moment and Its Political Afterlives*, Ohio: Ohio University Press.

Louro, Michele (2018) *Comrades Against Imperialism: Nehru, India, and Interwar Internationalism*, Cambridge: Cambridge University Press.

Luard, Evan (1982) *A History of the United Nations: Volume 1: The Years of Western Domination, 1945–1955*, London: Macmillan Press.

Luck, Edward C. (2008) 'A Council for All Seasons: The Creation of the Security Council and its Relevance Today' in Vaughan Lowe, Adam Roberts, Jennifer Welsh and Dominik Zaum (Eds.), *The United Nations Security Council and War: The Evolution of Thought and Practice Since 1945*, Oxford: Oxford University Press, pp. 61 - 85.

Macmillan, Margaret (2003) *Paris 1919: Six Months that Changed the World*, New York: Random House.

MacQueen, Norrie (2011) *Humanitarian Intervention and the United Nations*, Edinburgh: Edinburgh University Press.

Mahdavi, Mojtaba (2012) 'R2P in the Middle East and North Africa' in W. Andy Knight and Frazer Egerton (Eds.), *The Routledge Handbook of the Responsibility to Protect*, Abingdon: Routledge, pp. 257–275.

Mamlyuk, Boris (2017) 'Decolonization as a Cold War Imperative: Bandung and the Soviets' in Luis Eslava, Michael Fakhri and Vasuki Nesiah (Eds.), *Bandung,*

Global History, and International Law, Cambridge: Cambridge University Press, pp. 196–214.

Manela, Erez (2006) 'Imagining Woodrow Wilson in Asia: Dreams of East- West Harmony and the Revolt Against Empire in 1919', *American Historical Review*, Volume 111, Number 5, pp. 1327–1351.

Manela, Erez (2007) *The Wilsonian Moment: Self-Determination and the International Origins of Anticolonial Nationalism.* New York: Oxford University Press.

Massip, Roger (1955) 'Delegates from 29 African and Asian Countries Meet in Bandung' in *Le Figaro*, 18 April 1955, Available online: https://www.cvce.eu/en/obj/delegates_from_29_african_and_asian_countries_meet_in_bandung_from_le_figaro_18_april_1955-en-0abd33a5-e215-44fa-bfc5-756201f0b334.html. Accessed 12 April 2022.

Matz, Nele (2005) 'Civilization and the Mandate System Under the League of Nations as Origin of Trusteeship' in A. von Bogdandy and R. Wolfrum (Eds.), *Max Planck Yearbook of United Nations Law: Volume 9*, Leiden: Martinus Nijhoff, pp. 47–95.

Mayall, James (1991) 'Non-Intervention, Self-Determination and the "New World Order"', *International Affairs*, Volume 67, Number 3, pp. 421–429.

Mazower, Mark (2009) *No Enchanted Palace*, Princeton: Princeton University Press.

Mazower, Mark (2012) *Governing the World: The History of an Idea*, London: Allen Lane.

Morefield, Jeanne (2014) *Empires Without Imperialism: Anglo-American Decline and the Politics of Deflection*, New York: Oxford University Press.

Moses, Jeremy (2014) *Sovereignty and Responsibility: Power, Norms and Intervention in International Relations*, Basingstoke: Palgrave Macmillan.

Murray, Robert W. (2012) 'The Challenges Facing R2P Implementation' in W. Andy Knight and Frazer Egerton (Eds.), *The Routledge Handbook of the Responsibility to Protect*, Abingdon: Routledge, pp. 64–76.

Nehru, Jawaharlal (1955) 'World Peace and Cooperation', Available online: https://studylib.net/doc/18260402/jawaharlal-nehru--world-peace-and-cooperation--1955- Accessed 12 April 2022.

Nicholas, H.G. (1975) *The United Nations as a Political Institution (5th Edition)*, Oxford: Oxford University Press.

Nkrumah, Kwame (1965) *Neo-Colonialism: The Last Stage of Imperialism*, New York: International Publishers.

Orford, Anne (2006) 'A Jurisprudence of the Limit' in Anne Orford (Ed.), *International Law and Its Others*, Cambridge: Cambridge University Press, pp. 1–32.

Pahuja, Sundhya (2011) *Decolonising International Law: Development, Economic Growth and the Politics of Universality*, Cambridge: Cambridge University Press.

Parfitt, Rose (2011) '*Empire des Nègres Blancs*: The Hybridity of International Personality and the Abyssinia Crisis of 1935-1936', *Leiden Journal of International Law*, Volume 24, pp. 849–872.

Pasha, Mustapha Kamal (2016) 'The Bandung Within' in Phạm, Quỳnh N. and Robbie Shilliam (Eds.), (2016) *Meanings of Bandung: Postcolonial Orders and Decolonial Visions*, London: Rowman and Littlefield.

Patil, Vrushali (2008) *Negotiating Decolonization in the United Nations: Politics of Space, Identity and International Community*, Abingdon: Routledge.

Pedersen, Susan (2015) *The Guardians: The League of Nations and the Crisis of Empire*, Oxford: Oxford University Press.

Persaud, Randolph B. (2016) 'The Racial Dynamic in International Relations: Some Thoughts on the Pan-African Antecedents of Bandung' in Phạm, Quỳnh N. and Robbie Shilliam (Eds.), (2016) *Meanings of Bandung: Postcolonial Orders and Decolonial Visions*, London: Rowman and Littlefield.

Petersson, Fredrik (2014) 'Hub of the Anti-Imperialist Movement', *Interventions*, Volume 16, Number 1, pp. 49–71.

Phạm, Quỳnh N. and Robbie Shilliam (2016) 'Reviving Bandung' in Quỳnh N. Phạm and Robbie Shilliam (Eds.), *Meanings of Bandung: Postcolonial Orders and Decolonial Visions*, London: Rowman and Littlefield, pp 1–20.

Plummer, Brenda (1996) *Rising Wind: Black Americans and U.S. Foreign Affairs, 1935–1960*, Chapel Hill: University of North Carolina Press.

Plummer, Brenda (2003) 'Introduction' in Brenda Plummer (Ed.), *Window on Freedom: Race, Civil Rights and Foreign Affairs, 1945–1988*, Chapel Hill: University of North Carolina Press, pp. 1–20.

Prashad, Vijay (2007) *The Darker Nations: A People's History of the Third World*, London: The New Press.

Prashad, Vijay (2014) *The Poorer Nations: A Possible History of the Global South*, London: Verso.

Rajagopal, Balakrishnan (2003) *International Law From Below: Development, Social Movements and Third World Resistance*, Cambridge: Cambridge University Press.

Roberts, Adam (1993) 'Humanitarian War: Military Intervention and Human Rights', *International Affairs*, Volume 69, Number 3, pp. 429–449.

Roberts, Adam and Dominik Zaum (2008) *Selective Security: War and the United Nations Security Council Since 1945*, Abingdon: Routledge.

Rodney, Walter (2012 [1972]) *How Europe Underdeveloped Africa*, Cape Town: Pambazuka Press.

Roth, Brad R. (2011) *Sovereign Equality and Moral Disagreement: Premises of a Pluralist International Legal Order*, Oxford: Oxford University Press.

Rotmann, Philipp, Gerrit Kurtz and Sarah Brockmeier (2014) 'Major Powers and the Contested Evolution of a Responsibility to Protect', *Conflict, Security and Development*, Volume 14, Number 4, pp. 355–377.

Rowe, Edward T. (1971) 'The United States, The United Nations, and the Cold War', *International Organization*, Volume 25, Number 1, pp. 59–78.

Rutazibwa, Olivia (2010) 'The Problematics of the EU's Ethical (Self) Image in Africa: The EU as an 'Ethical Intervener' and the 2007 Joint Africa-EU Strategy', *Journal of Contemporary European Studies*, Volume 18, Number 2, pp. 209–228.

Rutazibwa, Olivia (2014) 'Studying Agaciro: Moving Beyond Wilsonian Interventionist Knowledge Production on Rwanda', *Journal of Intervention and Statebuilding*, Volume 8, Number 4, pp. 291–302.

Sabaratnam, Meera (2017) *Decolonising Intervention: International Statebuilding in Mozambique*, London: Rowman and Littlefield International.

Sayward, Amy L. (2013) 'International Institutions' in Richard H. Immerman and Petra Goedde (Eds.), *The Oxford Handbook of the Cold War*, Oxford: Oxford University Press.

Schlesinger, Stephen C. (2003) *Act of Creation: The Founding of the United Nations: A Story of Superpowers, Secret Agents, Wartime Allies and Enemies and Their Quest for a Peaceful World*, Boulder, Colorado, USA: Westview Press.

Seth, Sanjay (2013) 'Introduction' in Sanjay Seth (Ed.), *Postcolonial Theory and International Relations: A Critical Introduction*, Abingdon: Routledge, pp. 1–12.

Seybolt, Taylor (2008) *Humanitarian Military Intervention: The Conditions for Success and Failure*, Oxford: Oxford University Press.

Sherwood, Marika (1996) '"There is No New Deal for the Blackman in San Francisco": African Attempts to Influence the Founding Conference of the United Nations, April–July, 1945', *The International Journal of African Historical Studies*, Volume 29, Number 1, pp. 71–94.

Šimonović, Ivan (2019) 'Conclusion: R2P at a Crossroads: Implementation or Marginalization' in Cecilia Jacob and Martin Mennecke (Eds.), *Implementing the Responsibility to Protect: A Future Agenda*, London: Routledge, pp. 251–267.

Singham, Archie and Hune, Shirley (1986) 'The Non-Aligned Movement and World Hegemony', *The Black Scholar*, Volume 18, Number 2, pp. 48–57.

Steel, Ronald (1998) 'Prologue: 1919-1945-1989' in Manfred F. Boemeke, Gerald D. Feldman and Elisabeth Glaser (Eds.), *The Treaty of Versailles: A Reassessment After 75 Years*, Cambridge: Cambridge University Press, pp. 21–34.

Stein, Sabrina (2012) 'The UN and Genocide: A Comparative Analysis of Rwanda and the Former Yugoslavia' in Fulvio Attina (Ed.), *The Politics and Policies of Relief, Aid and Reconstruction*, Basingtoke: Palgrave Macmillan, pp. 173–190.

Stromseth, J., D. Wippman and Rosa Brooks (2006) *Can Might Make Rights?*, Cambridge: Cambridge University Press.

Sukarno (1955) 'Address Given by Sukarno – Bandung, 18th April 1955', Available online: http://www.cvce.eu/en/obj/address_given_by_sukarno_bandung_18_april _1955-en-88d3f71c-c9f9-415a-b397-b27b8581a4f5.html. Accessed 12 April 2022.

Tarazona, Liliana Obregon (2012) 'The Civilized and the Uncivilized' in Bardo Fassbender and Anne Peters (Eds.), *The Oxford Handbook of the History of International Law*, Oxford: Oxford University Press, pp. 917–938.

Taylor, Ian and Smith, Karen (2007) *United Nations Conference on Trade and Development (UNCTAD)*, London: Routledge.

Thakur, Ramesh (2006) *The United Nations, Peace and Security*, Cambridge: Cambridge University Press.

Thakur, Ramesh (2018) *Reviewing the Responsibility to Protect: Origins, Implementation and Controversies*, London: Routledge.

Tillery, Alvin B. (2011) *Between Homeland and Motherland: Africa, U.S. Foreign Policy, and Black Leadership in America*, New York: Cornell University Press.

Toye, John (2014) 'Assessing the G77: 50 Years after UNCTAD and 40 Years after the NIEO', *Third World Quarterly*, Volume 35, Number 10, pp. 1759–1774.

Trouillot, Michel-Rolf (1995) *Silencing the Past: Power and the Production of History*, Boston: Beacon Press.

Turner, Bryan (2006) *Vulnerability and Human Rights*, Pennsylvania: Pennsylvania State University.

Turner, W. Burghardt and Joyce Moore Turner (1988) *Richard B. Moore, Caribbean Militant in Harlem: Collected Writings 1920–1972*, London: Pluto Press.

Twitchett, Kenneth J. (1969) 'The Colonial Powers and the United Nations', *Journal of Contemporary History*, Volume 4, Number 1, pp. 167–185.

Van Hooft, Stan (2011) 'Humanity or Justice?', *Journal of Global Ethics*, Volume 7, Number 3, pp. 291–302.

Vitalis, Robert (2013) 'The Midnight Ride of Kwame Nkrumah and Other Fables of Bandung (Ban-doong)', *Humanity: An International Journal of Human Rights, Humanitarianism, and Development*, Volume 4, Number 2, pp. 261–288.

Waters, Malcolm (1996) 'Human Rights and the Universalization of Interests', *Sociology*, Volume 30, Number 3, pp. 593–600.

Weiss, Thomas G. (2012) *Humanitarian Intervention: War and Conflict in the Modern World*, Cambridge: Polity Press.

Welsh, Jennifer M. (2012) 'Who Should Act?: Collective Responsibility and the Responsibility to Protect' in W. Andy Knight and Frazer Egerton (Eds.), *The Routledge Handbook of the Responsibility to Protect*, Abingdon: Routledge, pp. 103–114.

Wheeler, Nicholas (2002) *Saving Strangers: Humanitarian Intervention in International Society*, Oxford: Oxford University Press.

Widodo (2015) 'Opening Statement', Asian-African Summit 2015, 22 April 2015, Available online: https://bandungspirit.org/IMG/pdf/jokowi-jakarta_opening_statement-220415-bsn.pdf. Accessed 12 April 2022.

Wilder, Gary (2015) *Freedom Time: Negritude, Decolonization and the Future of the World*, London: Duke University Press.

Wilson, Woodrow (1918) *President Woodrow Wilson's Fourteen Points*, Available online: http://avalon.law.yale.edu/20th_century/wilson14.asp. Accessed 12 April 2022.

Woocher, Lawrence (2012) 'The Responsibility to Prevent: Toward a Strategy' in W. Andy Knight and Frazer Egerton (Eds.), *The Routledge Handbook of the Responsibility to Protect*, Abingdon: Routledge, pp. 22–35.

Wright, Richard (1956) *The Color Curtain: A Report on the Bandung Conference*, New York: World Publishing Company.

Yifeng, Chen (2017) 'Bandung, China, and the Making of World Order in East Asia' in Luis Eslava, Michael Fakhri and Vasuki Nesiah (Eds.), *Bandung, Global History, and International Law*, Cambridge: Cambridge University Press, pp. 177–195.

PUBLISHED PAPERS

Asian-African Conference (1955) 'Final Communiqué of the Asian-African Conference', Available Online: https://www.cvce.eu/en/obj/final_communique_of_the_asian_african_con%20ference_of_bandung_24_april_1955-en-676237bd-72f7-471f-949a-88b6ae513585.html. Accessed 12 April 2022.

Asian-African Summit (2005) 'Declaration on the New Asian-African Strategic Partnership', Available online: https://bandungspirit.org/IMG/pdf/naaspcomplete-bandung_of_states_2005.pdf. Accessed 12 April 2022.

Asian-African Summit (2015) 'Declaration on Reinvigorating the New Asian-African Strategic Partnership', Available online: https://bandungspirit.org/IMG/pdf/decla-ration_on_reinvigorating_naasp.pdf. Accessed 12 April 2022.

Dumbarton Oaks (1944) 'Dumbarton Oaks: Washington Conversations on International Peace and Security Organization', Available online: http://www.jewishvirtuallibrary.org/jsource/ww2/dumbarton.html. Accessed 12 April 2022.

G77 (1964) *Joint Declaration of the Seventy-Seven Developing Countries Made at the Conclusion of the United Nations Conference on Trade and Development, Geneva, 15th June 1964*, Available online: https://www.g77.org/doc/Joint%20Declaration.html. Accessed 12 April 2022

G77 (1997) *San Jose Declaration and Plan of Action on South-South Trade, Investment and Finance, San Jose, Costa Rica, 13–15 January 1997*, Available online: https://www.g77.org/doc/sjdocs.html. Accessed 12 April 2022

International Commission on Intervention and State Sovereignty (2001) 'The Responsibility to Protect: Report on the International Commission on Intervention and State Sovereignty', Available online: https://idl-bnc-idrc.dspacedirect.org/bitstream/handle/10625/18432/IDL-18432.pdf?sequence=6&isAllowed=y. Accessed 12 April 2022.

League of Nations (1919) 'The Covenant of the League of Nations', Available online: http://avalon.law.yale.edu/20th_century/leagcov.asp. Accessed 12 April 2022.

Non-Aligned Movement (1961) *1st Summit Conference of Heads of State or Government of the Non-Aligned Movement, Belgrade, Serbia 6 September 1961* Available online: http://cns.miis.edu/nam/documents/Official_Document/1st_Summit_FD_Belgrade_Declaration_1961.pdf. Accessed 12 April 2022

Non-Aligned Movement (1964) *2nd Summit Conference of Heads of State or Government of the Non-Aligned Movement, Cairo, Egypt, 10 September 1964*, Available online: http://cns.miis.edu/nam/documents/Official_Document/2nd_Summit_FD_Cairo_Declaration_1964.pdf. Accessed 12 April 2022

Non-Aligned Movement (1970) *3rd Summit Conference of Heads of State or Government of the Non-Aligned Movement, Lusaka, Zambia, 8–10 September 1970*, Available Online: http://cns.miis.edu/nam/documents/Official_Document/3rd_Summit_FD_Lusaka_Declaration_1970.pdf. Accessed 12 April 2022

Non-Aligned Movement (1973) *4th Summit Conference of Heads of State or Government of the Non-Aligned Movement, Algiers, Algeria, 5–9 September 1973*, Available online: http://cns.miis.edu/nam/documents/Official_Document/4th_Summit_FD_Algiers_Declaration_1973_Whole.pdf. Accessed 12 April 2022

Non-Aligned Movement (1989) *9th Summit Conference of Heads of State or Government of the Non-Aligned Movement, Belgrade, Serbia, 4–7 September 1989*, Available online: http://cns.miis.edu/nam/documents/Official_Document/9th_Summit_FD_Belgrade_Declaration_1989_Whole.pdf. Accessed 12 April 2022

Non-Aligned Movement (2011) *16th Ministerial Conference and Commemorative Meeting of the Non-Aligned Movement, Bali, Indonesia 23–27 May 2011*, Available online: http://cns.miis.edu/nam/documents/Official_Document/16Summit-Final _Whole-Edited.pdf. Accessed 12 April 2022

UNCTAD (2022) 'About', Available online: https://unctad.org/ Accessed 12 April 2022.

United Nations (1945) 'Charter of the United Nations and Statute of the International Court of Justice', Available online: http://treaties.un.org/doc/Publication/CTC/ uncharter.pdf. Accessed 11 April 2022.

United Nations (1960) 'Declaration on the Granting of Independence to Colonial Countries and Peoples', Available Online: https://documents-dds-ny.un.org/doc/ RESOLUTION/GEN/NR0/152/88/PDF/NR015288.pdf?OpenElement Accessed 12 April 2022.

United Nations (1997) 'Renewing the United Nations: a Programme for Reform: Report of the Secretary-General', Available online: https://digitallibrary.un.org/ record/245922?ln=en. Accessed 12 April 2022.

United Nations (2005) '2005 World Summit Outcome', Available online: http://www .un.org/womenwatch/ods/A-RES-60-1-E.pdf. Accessed 12 April 2022.

United Nations (2022a) 'Preparatory Years: UN Charter History', https://www.un.org /en/about-us/history-of-the-un/preparatory-years. Accessed 12 April 2022.

United Nations (2022b) 'UN General Assembly Votes to Suspend Russia from the Human Rights Council', 7 April 2022, Available online: https://news.un.org/en/ story/2022/04/1115782. Accessed 12 April 2022.

United Nations General Assembly (1946) 'Verbatim Record of the First Plenary Meeting, Central Hall, Westminster, London, Thursday, 10th January 1946, at 4pm' (A/PV.1), Available online: http://www.un.org/Depts/dhl/landmark/pdf/a -pv1.pdf. Accessed 30 October 2013.

United Nations Security Council (2011) 'Resolution 1973', Available online: https:// documents-dds-ny.un.org/doc/UNDOC/GEN/N11/268/39/PDF/N1126839.pdf ?OpenElement. Accessed 11 April 2022.

United States (1944) *Dumbarton Oaks Documents on International Organization*, Available online: http://www.idaillinois.org/cdm/ref/collection/isl3/id/12662 Accessed 12 April 2022.

ARCHIVAL DOCUMENTS

League against Imperialism Archive

1. *Invitation to the International Congress against Colonial Oppression and Imperialism*, ARCH00804.1, League Against Imperialism Archive, International Institute of Social History (Amsterdam).

2. *Congress Manifesto*, ARCH00804.10, League Against Imperialism Archive, International Institute of Social History (Amsterdam).

3. *Second Anti-Imperialist World Congress – 'The Trade Unions and the Struggle Against Imperialism*, ARCH00804.89, League Against Imperialism Archive, International Institute of Social History (Amsterdam).
4. *Speech of Vasconcelias, Congress Meeting of February 10th, 1927*, ARCH00804.39, League Against Imperialism Archive, International Institute of Social History (Amsterdam).

United Nations Archives

1. *Letter from T. T. McCrosky to Mr Ojike*, May 30th, 1945, United Nations Conference on International Organisation – Outgoing Letters – Negroes (S-0596-0009-0017), United Nations Archives.
2. *Letter from Alger Hiss to Mr Moore*, June 1st, 1945, United Nations Conference on International Organisation – Outgoing Letters – Minorities (S-0596-0009-0011), United Nations Archives.
3. *Letter from Alger Hiss to Mrs Pandit*, May 11th, 1945, United Nations Conference on International Organisation – Outgoing Letters – Minorities (S-0596-0009-0011), United Nations Archives.
4. *Letter from T. T McCrosky to Mr Patty*, May 23rd, 1945, United Nations Conference on International Organisation – Outgoing Letters – Minorities (S-0596-0009-0011), United Nations Archives.
5. *Letter from T. T. McCrosky to Mr Batkus*, May 6th, 1945, United Nations Conference on International Organisation – Outgoing Letters – Minorities (S-0596-0009-0011), United Nations Archives.
6. *Letter from T. T. McCrosky to Mrs Black*, May 21st, 1945, United Nations Conference on International Organisation – Outgoing Letters – Negroes (S-0596-0009-0017), United Nations Archives.
7. *Remarks of Delegate of Australia at Ninth Meeting of Committee III/I*, May 17th, 1945, United Nations Conference on International Organisation – Files by Country – Australia UNCIO 1945 (S-0596-0003-0001), United Nations Archives.
8. *Summary Report of Fourth Meeting of Committee III/3*, May 10th, 1945, United Nations Conference on International Organisation – Files by Country - United States UNCIO 1945 (S-0596-0008-0003), United Nations Archives.
9. *Summary Report of 19th Meeting of Committee III/1*, June 12th, 1945, United Nations Conference on International Organisation – Secretary-General Speeches and Statements – Membership UNCIO 1945 (S-0596-0001-0010), United Nations Archives.
10. *Address by Minister of Foreign Affairs of Columbia at the Fifth Plenary Session*, April 30th, 1945, United Nations Conference on International Organisation – Organisation of Conference – United Nations Conference

on International Organisation UNCIO 1945 (S-0596-0002-0008), United Nations Archives.

11. *Corrigendum to Summary Report of Sixth Meeting of Committee III/3*, May 14th, 1945, United Nations Conference on International Organisation - Files by Country - United States UNCIO 1945 (S-0596-0008-0003), United Nations Archives.

12. *Remarks by Senator Connally, Delegate of the United States, at the Meeting of Commission III*, June 20th, 1945, United Nations Conference on International Organisation – Files by Country - United States UNCIO 1945 (S-0596-0008-0003), United Nations Archives.

13. *Summary of Fourth Meeting of Committee II/4*, May 14th, 1945, United Nations Conference on International Organisation - Files by Country – United States UNCIO 1945 (S-0596-0008-0003), United Nations Archives.

14. *Amendments of the Soviet Delegation to the United States Draft on Trusteeship System,* May 11th, 1945, United Nations Conference on International Organisation – Files by Country – U.S.S.R UNCIO 1945 (S-0596-0007-0014), United Nations Archives.

15. *Corrigendum to Verbatim Minutes of Third Meeting of Commission II*, June 20th, 1945, United Nations Conference on International Organisation – Files by Country – United Kingdom UNCIO 1945 (S-0596-0007-0016), United Nations Archives.

Bandung Archive

1. *Agenda Compiled by the Joint Secretariat of the Asian-African Conference*, April 16, 1955, HPPPDA, PRC FMA 207-00015-01, 11.

2. *Cable from the Chinese Embassy in Indonesia, 'What the United States is Doing in Indonesia prior to the Asian-African Conference'*, March 25, 1955, HPPPDA, PRC FMA 207-00002-04, 136–18.

3. *Summary of the Talks between Premier Zhou and Nehru and U Nu,* April 16, 1955, HPPPDA, PRC FMA 207-00015-01, 1–10.

4. *Report from the Chinese Foreign Ministry, 'Comments on the Asian-African Conference from Capitalist Ruled Countries After the Asian-African Conference',* May 10, 1955, HPPPDA, PRC FMA 207-00059-01.

Index

Africa, 60; European colonisation in, 52; North, 1, 116, 139, 142, 144. *See also* Asia-Africa alliance

African Academy of Arts and Research: NAACP conference with, 62; at UNCIO, 60

African Students Association, joint letter to UN, 60

Algeria: Algiers, 109; France relation to, 99

Angel, Zuleta, on sovereignty, 74–75

Anghie, Antony: on dynamic of difference, 73, 75, 80; on international law, 24–25; on sovereignty, 29

Annan, Kofi: *Renewing the United Nations* by, 114; on UN humanitarian intervention, 134, 137–38

anti-capitalism, 52–54; anti-colonialism relation to, 55; League against Imperialism as, 56; NIEO as, 108; Soviet Union, 100

anti-colonial resistance: anti-capitalist relation to, 52–54, 55; Asia-Africa alliance, 85; at Bandung Conference, 89–91, 93–94, 96–101; in global south, 57–58; Paris as hub for, 49–50; Soviet Union expressing,

78–79, 82, 100; to UN, 56, 58–60, 87; UNCTAD relation to, 109; to UN Security Council, 64

Appeal on Behalf of the Caribbean Peoples, Hiss response to, 61

Arab Spring, as anti-government protests, 1, 139

Archaeology of Knowledge (Foucault), 7

archives: anti-colonial, 8–9; colonialism in UN, 57; narratives produced through, 6–8, 149

Asia-Africa alliance: anti-colonialism of, 85; shared experience of, 88–89; Soviet Union relation to, 100; Third World Project relation to, 101; in UN General Assembly, 105. *See also* Bandung Conference (1955); New Asian-African Strategic Partnership

Asia-Africa Summit. *See* Bandung Conference (1955)

Asian states: US relation to, 92–93. *See also* Asia-Africa alliance

Atlantic Charter (1941), signing of, 18

Australia, 70–71

Bali, Indonesia, Non-Aligned Movement conference, 112

Bandung Conference: anti-colonialism at, 13, 85, 96–101, 150; Asia-Africa

167

4–5, 12, 15; as paternal figures, 68,
73, 86–87; political interests of,
127, 132–33; sovereign equality
undermined by, 69, 74–75; voting
procedure of, 2, 69–72
Persaud, Randolph B., on anti-colonial
activists, 50
Petioni, Charles A., 61
Phạm, Quỳnh N., on international
relations, 102, 151
Plummer, Brenda, on UN debates, 59
Portugal, NATO relation to, 96
postcolonial power: neocolonial
technologies of power compared to,
3–4, 144; sovereignty relation to, 34
postcolonial theory: colonial narratives
disrupted by, 3, 4–5; Western
liberalism in, 151
poverty: redistribution of wealth to
eliminate, 101, 113–14; as threat to
world peace, 108–9, 110–11
Prashad, Vijay, on neoliberalism, 111
protests, anti-government, Arab Spring
as, 1, 139–40

R2P. *See* Responsibility to Protect
rebuilding, after intervention, 136–37
redistribution, of resources. *See*
reparations
reform, UN, 118–19; Bandung
Conference for, 93, 97–100, 116–17;
Non-Aligned Movement for, 106–7,
110, 112–13; *Renewing the United
Nations* as, 114; Security Council,
67, 115, 116–18, 125, 142, 152;
UNCTAD for, 109
refugees, R2P relation to, 142
regime change, R2P to justify, 139
Renewing the United Nations report
(Annan), 114–15
reparations, for colonialism, 101, 111,
112–14, 117
resolutions, UN: Resolution 912, 133;
Resolution 1514, 103–4; Resolution
1973, 1, 139

responsibility: colonialism relation to,
143, 147, 148, 149; rhetoric of, 102,
110, 119, 122, 125, 132, 140, 151;
sovereignty relation to, 135–36,
144; UN Security Council power as,
72–75, 83
Responsibility to Protect (R2P):
adoption of, 1, 14; colonial power
dynamics perpetuated by, 144, 147;
as institutionalisation of privilege,
150; intervention in, 112, 121, 134–
37, 139; as neocolonialism, 14, 121,
138, 143–44, 148; as paternalism,
132, 135; sovereignty relation to,
5, 143–44; UN Security Council
relation to, 140–42
Rights of Man and Citizen (1789), 130
Rodney, Walter: on colonialism, 52; on
white supremacy, 108
Roosevelt, Franklin D.: Atlantic Charter
signed by, 18; Churchill meeting
with, 16; UN relation to, 22, 38, 64
Russia: invasion of Ukraine, 152;
UN Security Council veto by, 2,
133, 140, 152. *See also* permanent
members, UN Security Council;
Soviet Union
Rutazibwa, Olivia, on development, 135
Rwanda: genocide in, 133; selective
enforcement from, 137–38

Sabaratnam, Meera, on Eurocentrism,
5, 11
San Francisco, California. *See* United
Nations Conference on International
Organization (UNCIO)
Second World War: as League of
Nations failure, 20–21, 31, 57, 63;
UN formation after, 16, 17, 37–38;
US involvement in, 38, 64; won by
UN sponsoring nations, 22
Security Council, UN, 82; action in
Libya, 1; Bandung Conference
critique of, 98; Cold War effect
on, 100, 110, 125–26; equality